Take Me To Your Readers

*How to use the best children's books
to lead students to read, read, read*

Larry Swartz

Pembroke Publishers Limited

© 2017 Pembroke Publishers
538 Hood Road
Markham, Ontario, Canada L3R 3K9
www.pembrokepublishers.com

Distributed in the U.S. by Stenhouse Publishers
PO Box 11020
Portland, ME 04104-7020
www.stenhouse.com

Library and Archives Canada Cataloguing in Publication

Swartz, Larry, author
    Take me to your readers : how to use the best children's books to lead students to
read, read, read / Larry Swartz.

Issued in print and electronic formats.
ISBN 978-1-55138-326-2 (softcover).--ISBN 978-1-55138-927-1 (PDF)

    1. Literacy--Study and teaching (Elementary). 2. Children--Books and reading.
I. Title.

LB1576.S93 2017   372.6'044   C2017-903701-3
                                            C2017-903702-1

Editor: Kat Mototsune
Cover Design: John Zehethofer
Typesetting: Jay Tee Graphics Ltd.

Printed and bound in Canada
9 8 7 6 5 4 3 2 1

MIX
Paper from
responsible sources
FSC® C004071

Contents

Foreword

Increasingly, teachers are challenged to prepare students for an exploding array of literacy practices within a digitally connected world. Works on new literacies and nonprint media urge teachers to build on students' social media experiences, interests, and knowledge in order to make literacy instruction relevant to them and their lives.

But teachers' questions about supporting students' motivation and self-confidence as readers and viewers have not disappeared, nor have teachers stopped asking about effective teaching of vocabulary and content knowledge. Many continue to wonder about ways to support students' comprehension and writing, and to deepen students' appreciation for diverse perspectives and ways of living. As the questions endure, so does one answer: use literature. Within a connected and globalized world, literature in any form continues to have a primary place in classroom teaching and learning for motivating readers/viewers, for teaching cognitive aspects of reading/viewing, and for introducing diverse perspectives that lead to responsible citizenship in creating a more socially just world. Consideration must be given to selecting appropriate literature and designing meaningful activities for students to engage with and learn through the literature. In this book, Larry Swartz helps teachers with the challenge of bringing literature into classrooms.

I have come to know Larry as one of the leading Canadian educators in children's literature and look to him for recommendations on must-read books. In office conversations and while on our way to Canadian Children's Book Centre meetings, hours fly by as we talk about children's literature we have read and loved (and in some cases, have not loved). As children's literature aficionados, we have co-authored two books on teaching with children's literature: *Good Books Matter* and *This Is a Great Book!* Here, Larry invites educators, including those he once taught in teacher education courses, as well as librarians and authors, to join in the conversation. Through classroom stories, details of recommended practices, and titles representing a wide range of genres. Here, Larry and guest authors present exciting ways to mine the possibilities of engaging with literature in our classrooms.

— Shelley Stagg Peterson

Introduction

"Take out your readers!" I remember my Grade 4 teacher instructing the class, many years ago, as if a reader was something hidden within, some literary spirit we would need to "take out" to enter into the book world. My elementary education was in the 1950s and much of our reading was from anthology books, aka *readers*. The children's literature industry has, of course, exploded since the days of Dick and Jane and High Flight, and the literacy world has come to recognize that to help build real readers we need to offer them real books. In my youth there wasn't a Judy Blume, Rick Riordan, Dav Pilkey, J.K. Rowling, Eric Walters, or Mo Willems to delve into.

I was at the beginning of my career when attention was being paid to literature-based "whole-language instruction," and very early in my teaching I became hooked into connecting my students with good books. I believed (and still do) that with literature we can take our students to the whole world and bring the whole world into our classrooms. I was on a mission to seek out good books, and learned about them from taking courses, from journals, from dedicated visits to The Children's Book Store, and from book talks with Marion Seary, Judy Sarick, and Maria Martella.

Maria, owner of Tinlids Books, has remained a reliable and steadfast friend regarding good books. At a 2017 conference for librarians and teacher-librarians I greeted Maria and smiled when I saw the button badge she was wearing: Take Me To Your Reader. Very clever. Maria, being the friend she is, passed on the button as a gift and, as I wandered through the alleys and lanes of the book displays, the words sang through my head. A few weeks later, I asked Maria if I could borrow the title for a new book I was writing. "Absolutely!" she assented. I am grateful to Maria for allowing me this title, for I feel that my mission throughout my career has been to find teachers who seek out ways to take me to their readers: to find a title to share as a read-aloud; to find ways turn students into book lovers; to learn about strategies that use literature to support curriculum.

Take Me To Your Readers has provided me the opportunity to shine a spotlight on instructional strategies that use children's literature in the classroom. When presenting workshops or having conversations in school hallways, I approach friends and colleagues and ask, "Tell me about a best practice you've implemented in your literacy program." The answers appear as Guest Voices, through which teachers from a range of grade levels reflect on classroom events that use

More than 30 years ago, I listened to Frank Smith conclude a speech with words that have been on my shoulder throughout my teaching:
If literacy is going to live, it is going to live in our classrooms.
If it is going to die, it is going to die in our classrooms.

books to help meet curriculum expectations and engage readers. *Take Me To Your Readers* also encouraged me to demonstrate how literature can be used in the classroom. The chance to visit classrooms (Larry visits…) provided research opportunities and allowed me to work with students and gather data for several units in this book. Ultimately, I was able to look into the rearview mirror of my teaching to describe and celebrate and reflect upon significant events that have been essential to my teaching repertoire. Highlighting these events helped me share my personal practices from Grades 2 through 8 over 25 years (Larry's Class). Writing about these lessons and units helped me to consider my own best practices, the ones that have informed and shaped my work as a teacher, consultant, author, and university instructor.

When meeting teachers in courses and workshops, I am often asked, "What new books are you recommending?" and "How do you 'use' these books?" Answering those two questions is the heart of this resource. I also believe that meaningful strategies that encourage active, interactive learning through talk, writing, and the arts are important in sharpening comprehension skills, promoting meaningful response, and demonstrating that reading is personal and that each reader is unique.

In our digital world—where we probably read more than ever before—I hold on to the belief that great books matter as a balance to our onscreen time. For Shelley Stagg Peterson, the word *great* denotes a book that will have significant impact on a young reader, that will stay with the reader long after it has been returned to the shelf. For author John Green, "Great books help you understand and they help you feel understood." The ability to say, "This is a great book!" depends on the child, the context, the culture, and the occasion. I believe that, as educators, we can help young people develop as readers. Our students may become lifelong readers because of what we have done in our classrooms—or not. I recognize that not all students will choose to read good books into their adolescent years and beyond but, for the time they are with us in schools, we help students understand that reading can be an enjoyable and rich endeavor. Reading is indeed a lifelong process, but it is our responsibility, challenge, and joy to make reading come alive in our classrooms by introducing our students to good literature, by implementing engaging response modes, and, most of all, by demonstrating our own passion for reading.

It is my intention that this resource will encourage teachers to consider their own best practices and to learn from the practice of others. I offer teachers book titles and authentic practices, and suggestions how to take them to their readers, to lead those readers to want to read, read, read.

Using this Book

The five chapters in this book provide an organizing framework for using children's literature in the classroom. In each chapter, there are one or two instructional strategies provided, drawn from classroom practice to engage students with literature. Though a specific text is used as a context for the learning, the suggested strategies can be applied to most any book used in the classroom. It is recommended that teachers use this book by considering a chapter topic of choice and/or choosing from a menu of instructional strategies. Choice, based on student needs and interests, and on consideration of implementing curriculum outcomes, is central to the practical applications of this resource.

Chapters

Each chapter is introduced by a list of statements to help teachers reflect upon and plan a program that leads students to read.

Take Me to Your Readers offers a structure for sharing ideas and strategies for planning and implementing a program that promotes a love of reading.

1. Connected by Books
   - Being passionate about sharing books with students
   - Exercising and monitoring choice
   - Motivating a community of readers
2. Connected by Genre
   - Exploring types of writing with the intention of coming to understand the medium and the message
   - Considering the use of a number of genre forms (e.g., picture books, novels, poetry, etc.) and functions (e.g., persuasion, explanation, opinion, etc.)
   - Connecting reading and writing contexts
3. Connected by Response
   - Allowing readers to open up text for interpretation and reflection
   - Using a variety of modes to represent and reveal inside-the-head thoughts
   - Extending comprehension by having readers collaborate with a partner, in small groups, as a whole class.
4. Connected by Theme
   - Organizing a multidisciplinary, multi-genre program
   - Tapping into the needs and interests of the students
   - Encouraging a range of research and response connected to a variety of curriculum areas
5. Connected to Curriculum
   - Using children's literature to support all subjects (e.g., mathematics, science, social studies, history, the arts)
   - Using fiction and nonfiction resources to activate prior knowledge and build inquiry
   - Including reading, writing, the arts, and technology and media as means of responding creatively and critically to a text

Strategies

All strategies are designated by the 📚 icon.

Take Me to Your Readers is intended to provide teachers with an overview of best practices in classrooms for literacy teaching using children's literature. Each of the strategies outlined in the book is drawn from real classroom experiences, under the following three headings:

Larry's Class

These lessons have been an important part of my language-arts classroom practice from Grades 2–8 over a 25-year span. I have also had the opportunity to conduct research in response to literature and present these findings in a thesis entitled *Text Talk: Towards an Interactive Classroom Model for Encouraging, Supporting and Promoting Literacy* (2000).

Larry Visits Classrooms

Many teachers welcomed me into their classrooms to share literature and demonstrate an instructional strategy with their students. A visit into the classroom helped me gather student samples to serve as data for the learning event.

Guest Voices

This book includes overviews of lessons and strategies from teacher candidates, experienced teachers, occasional teachers, librarians, special education teachers, and English Language Learning teachers. Each was eager to contribute to the book by identifying an instructional strategy, describing an activity they implemented with their students, and reflecting on the learning. It was particularly rewarding that a number of these voices included current classroom teachers who were once candidates in the teacher-education literacy courses I taught at OISE (Ontario Institute for Studies in Education).

Bookshelf

Lists of recommended titles of children's literature have been included throughout the book to support the content of a particular unit. The majority of these picture books, novels, poetry, scripts, and nonfiction resources fill my personal bookshelves. I am grateful to colleagues and classroom teachers who recommended favorite resources, and to lists found on blogs, to augment my lists.

Teaching Tips

Reproducible masters have been offered to facilitate the implementation of a number of learning strategies.

Lists throughout the book offer a menu of suggestions to consider when organizing a balanced literacy program that is framed by children's literature. There are, as well, tips for implementing a learning strategy successfully.

Acknowledgments

- David Booth for the advice and the teaching.
- Maria Martella, owner of Tinlids, for all the books over all the years. And a loud shout-out for inspiring the title of this book!
- Shelley Stagg Peterson, colleague and friend who is a great partner to talk about (and write about) great books. Thanks, too, for the inspiring words welcoming readers to this book.
- Charlotte Teeple and friends at the Canadian Children's Book Centre for inviting me into the book awards family.
- The *Reading for the Love of It* Committee. The RFTLOI conference is an important annual touchstone for me. Thank you for the Spreading the Joy of Reading honor.
- The educators who chose to share their best practices for this publication.
- The teachers who invited me into their classrooms as a guest instructor. Moreover, thanks to their students who shared their responses with me. I learned a lot.

Connected by Books

I'm not the same reader when I finish a book as I was when I started. Brains are tangle of pathways, and reading creates new ones. Every book changes your life. So I like to ask: How is this book changing mine?

—Will Schwalbe, *Books for Living*

Our goal as teachers of reading is ultimately to build lifelong readers. Our classrooms can set a foundation for inspiring a love of books. Many of the students in our classes will learn to make fictional reading part of their lives. Many will not. Many will come to understand the importance of reading for knowledge and for enjoyment because of us, or in spite of us. Most will come to read, but perhaps not the stuff we expect them to. If we believe that books matter, we need to provide the best quality literature and be a cheerleader for the power of reading good books.

As teachers, we can share our own reading tastes with students; display reading posters; read aloud to students; take students to the school library; arrange visits to local bookstores and community libraries; encourage book purchases from book fairs and book clubs; create a classroom-as-book-club; provide opportunities for a wide range of responses; respond wisely to student responses; talk about books; write about books; buy books; display books; taste, chew, and devour books. If we really want to lead students to want to read, read, read, we need to be passionate about our goal of including books in significant ways in our literacy programs. In no particular order, we need to

- Provide time for reading aloud to students
- Provide a time for independent leisure reading in our programs
- Take the initiative to investigate, talk about, buy new books for the classroom
- Provide opportunities for authentic responses
- Find balance in the program where students have choice in their reading and modes of response
- Recognize that reading is not going to just happen in a reading program
- Make the classroom a book club, a community of readers that talks about books critically

For Your Consideration

- ☐ Are students excited about the reading program in your class?
- ☐ Does each student feel successful in their reading progress?
- ☐ Is daily reading aloud an important component of your reading program?
- ☐ How significant is choice of books in your reading program?
- ☐ How do you choose the books for your literacy program?
- ☐ Do you, as a teacher, talk about your personal reading?
- ☐ How satisfied are you with your classroom library? How might you enrich it?
- ☐ Do you provide opportunities for students to use the school library?
- ☐ Is there a balance of whole-class, small-group, and independent reading experiences in your classroom?
- ☐ How would you describe the independent reading program in your classroom?
- ☐ How successfully do you support the range of readers in your classroom? The independent reader? The reluctant reader? The struggling reader?
- ☐ Is consideration given to both boy and girl readers in the classroom?
- ☐ How do you motivate and celebrate reading in your classroom?
- ☐ Have you successfully established a partnership between school and home reading?

Crawling into a Book with Thirty Children: When the Teacher Reads Aloud

No matter the grade level, when we are asking our kids to enter into a genre that will demand more from them in terms of careful thought and when they are "listening up" in terms of sophistication of the story, outstanding instruction will be required if we are, in fact, going to captivate the entire group rather than just a few bright stars.
—Steven L. Layne, *In Defense of Read Aloud: Sustaining Best Practice*

Reading aloud and talking about what we're reading sharpens children's brains.

— Mem Fox, *Reading Magic*

Many, but not all, of children's first encounters with books in their homes and schools are while listening to a caring adult reading aloud to them. It doesn't matter if the adult is a parent, relative, babysitter, librarian, or early-years teacher; young children often become engaged with the book, looking at the illustrations and hearing the cadences of the poem, story, or informational text being read aloud. The pleasure of enjoying a book with someone significant in their lives can continue throughout the school years. Teachers can build on the expectations established in many children's preschool years by reading aloud daily to students of any age.

We know that most primary teachers read aloud picture books to their classes. Students in Grades 3 to 6 also listen to picture books read aloud, but are most likely to have novels or parts of novels read aloud to them. For a balanced literacy program, it is also important for teachers of Grades 7 to 9 to continue the important practice of reading aloud. When teachers choose titles to read aloud, a range of motivations is at work. For many teachers, the choice is practical. There may be only a single copy of a novel readily available. Or a teacher might be so keen on a book that he or she wants to present it as a community read, even though some students may choose to read the book on their own. Then again, the teacher might want to introduce and share a classic. Books such as *Charlotte's Web* by E.B. White, *The Little Prince* by Antoine de Saint Exupéry, *Mr. Popper's Penguins* by Richard and Florence Atwater, and *The Wind in the Willows* by Kenneth Grahame have been popular read-aloud choices for several generations.

Ten Tips for Reading Aloud a Picture Book

1. Although the books you choose to read aloud should be appropriate and relevant to the needs and wants of your listeners, choose titles that appeal to you, so you can share your enthusiasm with your audience.

2. Choose a title that listeners might not read independently. Following the read-aloud experience, students should be motivated to revisit and read the book on their own, and to read other titles by the author or other books in the genre or on a similar theme or topic.
3. Draw attention to the format. For picture books, encourage an examination of the illustrations, though all images should be shown for any book. Discuss how the illustrations enhance the verbal text. Does the story stand on its on without pictures?
4. Rehearse the stories you read.
5. Set a context for sharing the reading. Discuss the title, the cover illustration, the dedication page. Share information about the book and the author.
6. Before reading the book, activate prior knowledge and experience to motivate listeners to make connections. Invite them to make predictions by examining the cover page or the lead page. Take a picture walk through the book, discussing how the visual images tell a story.
7. Develop performance strategies that invite listeners into the story. Use dynamic shifts in volume and fluctuations in your tone of voice. Develop character voices that can be used to bring the story alive dramatically.
8. Find places to pause and ask questions or make observations. Invite spontaneous discussion from the whole class, or have listeners turn-and-talk to respond to a question.
9. Use the think-aloud process. Tell listeners what is going on inside your head as you read the book out loud. This is a useful demonstration of strategies that good readers use to make meaning of a text. Students can witness you as a reader, not just a teacher.
10. You can usually finish the reading of a picture book aloud at one sitting. On some occasions, you might read part of the book and invite oral or written, artistic or drama response. It is also appropriate and important to reread a title after an initial reading. There's no need to be satisfied with "We've already read this!" Revisiting, reviewing, and refocusing can lead to a deeper response. This rereading may happen within one week or at some later date.

Bookshelf: Books to Read Aloud

Early Years

Almost any text can be read aloud and shared with a community of readers. The books suggested here have served me well in my teaching and have proved to be favorites with students.

Cousins, Lucy. *Jazzy in the Jungle*
Feiffer, Jules. *Bark, George*
Fox, Mem; illus. Julie Vivas. *Wilfred Gordon McDonald Partridge*
Jeffers, Oliver. *How to Catch a Star* (Also *The Long Way Back*)
Klassen, Jon. *I Want My Hat Back* (Also *This Is Not My Hat*; *We Found a Hat*)
Rosenthal, Amy Krouse; illus. Tom Lichtenheld. *Duck! Rabbit!*
Tullet, Herve. *Press Here* (Also *Mix It Up*)
Willems, Mo. *Knuffle Bunny* (Also *Don't Let the Pigeon Drive the Bus* series)

Picture Books

Baldacchino, Christine; illus. Isabelle Malenfant. *Morris Micklewhite and the Tangerine Dress* (French: *Boris Brindamour et la robe orange*)

Boelts, Maribeth; illus. Noah Z. Jones. *Those Shoes*
De la Peña, Matt; illus. Christian Robinson. *Last Stop on Market Street*
Daywalt, Drew; illus. Oliver Jeffers. *The Day the Crayons Quit* (Sequel: *The Day the Crayons Came Home*)
George, Angela May; illus. Owen Swan. *Out*
Hall, Kirsten; illus. Matthew Forsythe. *The Gold Leaf*
Henkes, Kevin. *Lily's Purple Plastic Purse*
John, Jory; illus. Lane Smith. *Penguin Problems*
Jonas, Ann. *Round Trip*
Maclear, Kyo; illus. Katty Maurey. *The Specific Ocean*
Ringtved, Glenn; illus. Charlotte Pardi. *Cry, Heart, But Never Break*
Rylant, Cynthia; illus. Brendan Wenzel. *Life*
Wild, Margaret; illus. Ron Brooks. *Fox*

Novels (Middle Years)

Applegate, Katherine. *The One and Only Ivan*
Brown, Peter. *The Wild Robot*
DiCamillo, Kate. *The Miraculous Journey of Edward Toulane* (Also *The Tale of Desperaux; The Magician's Elephant*)
Gardiner, John Reynolds. *Stone Fox*
Morpurgo, Michael. *War Horse*
Palacio, R.J. *Wonder*
Pennypacker, Sara. *Pax*
Spinelli, Jerry. *Maniac Magee* (Also *Wringer; The Warden's Daughter*)
Steig, William. *Abel's Island*
Walliams, David. *Mr. Stink*

📚 BOOK OF THE DAY/WEEK/MONTH/YEAR

Larry's Class

When I read to my students, I feel that I am modeling both fluent reading and a love of reading. I can introduce texts to my students that they might not otherwise encounter. Hearing a book read expands students' vocabulary and their familiarity with a variety of sentence structures and ideas. When I choose to read aloud a book, I feel it is important that I become familiar with the content of the text, and communicating my enthusiasm for the book carries me far in engaging students. The primary goal of reading aloud is to foster young people's enjoyment and understanding of the text. When questions are asked to encourage students to share their thoughts, the opportunity is given to deepen understanding, clarify difficult concepts or relationships, and encourage emotional response to the book. Books chosen to read aloud can be integrated into the curriculum and can lead to meaningful talk, writing, visual arts, or drama activities. By incorporating reading aloud as a significant ritual in my classroom, I help students develop their own tastes in books and consider personal choices of an author, a book in a series, a genre, or information about a topic offered by the read-aloud.

Book of the Day

A day did not go by that we did not share a picture book (sometimes two). To make comparisons between the books we've experienced as a community read-aloud, titles are recorded daily on a one-month calendar chart to create a Read-Aloud Calendar. This task is usually the responsibility of one student, whose job it is to copy the title of the book on a designated square of the week, providing a record of the five (or more) titles listened to in a week. The activity also invites students to share their opinions about these titles as they are asked to consider: "Why did you choose this book as a favorite?"

Book of the Week

At the end of the week, the class revisits the five titles, preferably with the books on display. A vote is held so that the class chooses a favorite. A star is placed beside this title.

Book of the Month

At the end of the month, the class votes for a favorite title by revisiting the four titles that have a star beside them. A circle is drawn around the monthly winner.

Read-alouds may include poetry, nonfiction selections, newspaper or magazine articles, announcements, etc. The activity could be developed to record a Poem of the Day. Imagine reading over 180 poems in one year!

Book of the Year

At the end of the year, it is rewarding to visit the ten Read-Aloud Calendars. Together we prepare a top-ten list of titles that can be shared with other teachers.

INTERACTIVE READ-ALOUDS

Larry visits Lise Hawkins' Grade 1 Classroom

Interactive read-alouds focus on comprehension; the read-aloud experience is enhanced because students are engaged in the reading process before, during, and after the experience. They involve students in the reading and help them become better listeners. Techniques may vary for stories, nonfiction, or poetry selections, but ultimately the goal is to demonstrate strategies to students—the strategies we use to make sense of a story. Interactive read-alouds allow a community of readers to reveal what is going on inside their heads as they listen to text being read aloud.

1. *Before Reading*: Introduce the book and pose a question that activates students' background knowledge or experiences.
2. *During Reading*: Engage students by pausing periodically during the reading to discuss what has been read. This is a meaningful way to help students make predictions, make connections, raise questions, etc. You can point out text features, explain vocabulary, focus on the way the verbal and nonverbal text conveys the meaning of the story. One of the most authentic techniques to use is to share what is going on insider your head as the reading unfolds, demonstrating how readers make sense of text.
3. *After Reading*: Opportunities are provided for students to respond to the book. This can be as simple as a think–pair–share conversation with a

partner, a whole-class discussion, or an activity that invites written, artistic, or dramatic responses.

Interactive techniques invite students to
- Make predictions at pivotal points in the story, perhaps confirming or revising predictions as story unfolds
- Share personal stories of what has happened to them or to someone they know
- Make connections to other books, media, or the world
- Visualize by describing what is going on inside their heads
- Share puzzlements and questions that may emerge, perhaps clarifying information to help readers make sense of what is being read
- Unpack the language and style used by the author
- Share their knowledge about a topic and learn new information shared by others
- Listen to the viewpoints of others

When a book title or syntactic pattern within a book is framed by a question or questions, it can be considered an ideal resource for reading aloud, since it invites interactive personal responses from reader and can initiate a sense of inquiry prompted by discussion.

What Color Is the Wind? by Anne Herbauts is the story of a little, blind giant who sets off on a journey to find answers to the question *What color is the wind?* Each of the animals and people he meets answers the little giant according to their experiences. The picture book is unique in its presentation of illustrations that includes glossy images, tactile textures, and cut-out shapes.

The following transcript provides an overview of student responses as *What Color Is the Wind?* by Anne Herbauts was read aloud. Of particular note are the questions the teacher asks to prompt thinking and the questions the children ask to prompt inquiry. At times, the teacher shares what is going on inside his head as he reads the book, demonstrating comprehension strategies that include visualization, questioning, and making connections. To begin, the title's question invites immediate responses that engaged the students.

Teacher: What color is the wind?

> Greyish
> Clear
> Bluish-whitish-silver kind of color
> The color of glass

Text: *The little giant sets out early to search for the wind and its color.*
Teacher: Why do you think this character wants to find out about the wind?

> Because he's blind?
> He can feel the wind. But he can't see it.
> The wind doesn't have color. How will he find an answer?

Text: *No, says the wolf, the wind is the dark smell of the forest.*

> I don't get it.
> How can the wind smell?

Teacher: Smell is another sense that we use. So the wolf doesn't tell the giant what he sees, but he describes how the wind smells to him.
Teacher: I'm wondering why the author repeated the word *Water* three times.

> (no response)

Text: *No, no the roots rumble... It is the color of sap and pomegranates.*

I think those red dots must be pomegranates?
What is sap?
I think sap is what bees eat from trees and flowers.
Sap is in a tree to make maple syrup.
Sap is the juice inside the tree.

Teacher (pointing to picture): I like the way the little giant has his eyes closed with a little smile. I'm wondering what he is thinking.

(no response)

Teacher: Can you predict what the last page is?

Only white.
(The last page *is* blank.)

Teacher: What did you like about this book?

It's calming.
It makes a lot of sense. A lot of colors are put in the book. There is more than one answer to the question.
There had to be different colors to teach us to see things.

To conclude, one story was shared:

I have an uncle who is blind. He has to listen very carefully to what is around him. He can hear very well.

Teacher: I wonder how we would answer your uncle if he asked, "What color is the wind?"

Bookshelf: Picture Books Framed by Questions

Gaarder, Jostein; illus. Akin Duezakin. *Questions Asked*
Burningham, John. *Would you rather...*
Harris, Annaka; illus. John Rowe. *I Wonder...*
Morstad, Julie. *Today*
Perry, Sarah. *If...*
Yamada, Kobi; illus. Mae Besom. *What do You Do With an Idea?* (Also *What Do You Do With A Problem?*)

A Community Reads:
When the Class Reads the Same Novel

When I began teaching, I was eager to introduce novels into my language arts program and went down the hall to see what was available in the cupboard for my Grade 7 students. And so I taught *Cheaper by the Dozen* by Frank Galbraith. Why this book? Fifty copies sat on the shelf. I took what I could get. I actually read it when I was younger and remembered it being funny. And so my class of 30 students embarked on a five-week program with a book that was somewhat humorous, somewhat sexist, and very dated. I persevered, because I had prepared questions for the students to answer after each chapter.

That was my first year of teaching. Then I took continuing education courses in language arts and, in my second year of teaching, I recognized the essential need to arrange the students in groups where students would have some choice. So I went back to the cupboard and gathered together ten copies of each of the following titles, each the first book in a trilogy: *The White Mountains* by John Christopher, *The Keeper of the Isis Light* by Monica Hughes, and *The Wizard of Earthsea* by Ursula Le Guin. The fact that all three titles were science fiction at least provided us with a community connection by genre. After a book talk, students were encouraged to choose the novel that interested them the most. I did have students respond to questions that I designed, but at least I was moving forward by having the chapters chunked, so students needed to respond only every three or perhaps four chapters. "Creative" activities involved dramatizing an event, designing a new book cover, and writing a logbook entry from a character's point of view.

My journey of teaching of reading evolved as I continued taking courses, attending professional development sessions, discussing my program with my colleagues and with a program consultant, and reading professional books about how to best teach reading. Upon reflection, I am fairly certain that I would not return to the whole-class novel. What if a student had already read the novel? Didn't want to read the novel? Didn't connect to the genre? Struggled to read the novel? Finished reading the novel in a matter of days? What if the novel I chose appealed mostly to boys? To girls?

Research informs us that a majority of novels read in middle-years classrooms are experienced as whole-class community novels: all students read the same book. There are certainly advantages to this method, mostly community building. It is, however, strongly encouraged that during the year teachers balance the program by facilitating group instruction and having each reading a different novel in pairs or, ideally, groups of five or six students. To help build the community and promote connections among group members, the choice of books should be organized around a focus: a theme, an author, or a genre. If we believe that our reading programs should develop a lifelong love of books, there needs to be a balance of instruction based on the strengths and challenges of whole-class novel study.

Whole-Class Reading of One Novel

Strengths	Challenges
• Minimal organization required • Easy to manage responses before, during, and after reading • Controllable monitoring and assessment of student responses	• Limited or minimal student choice • Does not address differences in student interest and ability • Requires control of reading experience (e.g., pacing)

Advice to beginning teachers on how to create a balanced novel program might encompass the following organization:

Term 1: Whole-Class Community Novel
Term 2: Reading in Small Groups (e.g., Literature Circles)
Term 3: Independent Reading

For more on Independent Reading initiatives see pages 23 and 28.

See When The Teacher Reads Aloud on page 12.

Disclaimer: I do read novels aloud over the year, a different kind of whole-class community experience. Reading aloud by the teacher should be ongoing and include all kinds of texts, including the novel. The novel we choose to read aloud provides an opportunity to demonstrate how we make sense of text. Writing, talk, and arts response events we choose to introduce should be centred on the novel. The novel read aloud by the teacher should also lead students to read more by the author, series, theme, or genre.

In 2015, sixty OISE teacher candidates embarked on an inquiry to how novels are being taught in Grades 6–8. The six most popular titles presented as whole-class community reading:

Elijah of Buxton by Christopher Paul Curtis
The Breadwinner by Deborah Ellis
The Outsiders by S.E. Hinton
The Giver by Lois Lowry
Hatchet by Gary Paulsen
Walking Home by Eric Walters

ORGANIZING A COMMUNITY READ

Guest Voice: Rute Laranjeiro, Grade 7 Teacher

Two Grade 7 teachers discuss their experiences with introducing a novel read by each member of the class. By answering some interview questions, the teachers were able to summarize and reflect upon the experience.

1. Why did you choose the novel *Roll Of Thunder, Hear My Cry?*

Roll of Thunder, Hear My Cry by Mildred D. Taylor, winner of the Newbery Medal in 1971, tells of racism during the Great Depression. Narrator Cassie Logan describes her school experiences, her family's survival in rural Mississippi, and the tension caused by a boycott organized by her mother when she learns that the Wallace family, owners of the local store, are responsible for the burning of three black men. This set of books includes *Let the Circle Be Unbroken* and *The Road to Memphis* (sequels) and *The Land* (prequel).

Black History Month was approaching, which raised my consciousness and desire to introduce literature that might help students understand the issue of racism. On a practical level, there were enough copies of the novel available for me to embark on a novel exploration with the whole class. Our first experience with a novel, therefore, was a community read in which each student would have his or her own copy of the book.

2. Can you highlight some organizational procedures that took place so that each student had an opportunity to read and respond to the book?

- I decided to divide the novel into chunks (about three chapters for each chunk). Three or four questions were posted on the class website for students to answer over a period of four or five days.
- I organized a weekly class discussion to discuss the novel in depth. The questions provided a framework for the discussion.
- Time was given in class for independent reading. Students were also required to read and respond to the novel outside of class time.
- A link was provided to an audio recording of the novel, which provided some students with an alternative way to experience the text.

3. Besides questioning, what was a response activity that invited the students to examine the book more closely?

Students were required to create a picture book, using words and pictures, that would either retell one of the events from the novel or invent a story connected to one of the themes (e.g., segregation). For example, one student created a book about two different-colored frogs who were forced to be separated.

4. What do you think the learning was with this unit?

The novel is a powerful narrative that is centred on segregation and prejudice. I am confident the book gave students the opportunity to consider the issue of racism from a historical perspective and as it applies to today's world. Also, I think with having everyone in the class read the same novel, they had an experience with a text that provided for a range of different opinions to be shared and respected.

5. What are some next steps for you to consider in teaching novels?

I think it's important for students to read other novels that support this theme. There are many books with Afro-American and Afro-Canadian protagonists and I intend to make these available for another novel unit for which students are divided into groups. I realized from the whole-class experience that students read at different paces and bring different background experiences to the text. By organizing small groups I recognize that students need choice in their reading based on skill development, interest, and social interactions. The fact that we will all be exploring the same theme allows me to structure the learning. This time, students will have choice in the groups that are formed. This will provide me with the opportunity to facilitate literature circles, which will promote a more focused exploration of a novel. There are several novels for this age group that give insights into the Underground Railroad experience; by facilitating this exploration I will give students the chance to not only gain information and insights into the Underground Railroad experience, but also to have the opportunity to engage with the genre of historical fiction.

Bookshelf: Books on Black Slavery

Curtis, Christopher Paul. *Elijah of Buxton*
Lester, Julius. *Day of Tears*
McCoy, Sarah. *The Mapmaker's Children*
Petry, Ann. *Harriet Tubman: Conductor of the Underground Railroad*
Pignat, Caroline. *The Gospel Truth*
Smucker, Barbara. *Underground to Canada*

Choice Matters: Helping Readers Choose the Right Book for Independent Reading

I value engagement more than a particular text, and helping students learn to make good choices rests on suggestion not coercion. I believe the only real and lasting interest in reading comes from engagement… the secret of my system, perhaps, is the accepted and encouraged diversity of the books that line my shelves.

— Penny Kittle, *Book Love*

Reading fiction carries you further into imagination and invention than you would be capable of on your own, takes you into other people's lives, and often, by reflection, deeper into your own. I will indulge a resounding tautology: every great civilization, including ours, has had a great literature and great readers. If literature matters less to young people than it once did, we are all in trouble.

— David Denby, *Lit Up*

In our classrooms, there is little good in teaching students to be readers if they are not going to be readers for life. A serious, deliberate classroom ritual is required to make this happen. Students need to be encouraged to read at their own pace, using materials they've chosen to read, during school time. Students need time for independent reading.

In classrooms, independent reading choices need to be made by the student, but teachers have a key role to play in promoting the activity. We can guide students and offer advice if needed, but ultimately students should be given the responsibility of deciding what they are going to read. Effective teachers can encourage choice by displaying a range of books in the classroom, encouraging use of the classroom and community library, and providing time in the program for independent reading. They set a consistent daily time for independent leisure reading, allowing 15 to 30 minutes, depending on the age of the students. Essentially, as students read for pleasure, they note how authors model good writing; the more they read, the greater the likelihood they will apply and practice reading strategies daily, enhancing their reading comprehension and achievement in reading.

The teaching of reading requires a recognition of choice, but initial choice begins with the teacher. How much choice do students have in the books they read? How much time can be designated to independent reading? Will there be a requirement for follow-up activities, or is it enough to just let them read? Teachers have different perceptions about the place of independent reading time in their reading programs. Some teachers, if the timetable allows, designate a specific daily ritual. Some introduce independent reading sporadically throughout the week or month. Others can't seem to find time to fit it all in. A further challenge is to consider when, how, and if students will be responding to their independent leisure reading through writing, talk, or the arts to give further data for assessment.

In *Good Choice: Supporting Independent Reading and Response, K–6*, Tony Stead says "independent reading needs to become an integral and focused component of a daily reading program, not simply an activity for early finishers for settling down after lunch." (2009, p. 4)

When we choose books to read on holiday, that sit on our bedside tables, or for our own leisure reading, we probably don't want anyone telling us, "This is the book you must read." We want choice. So do our students. In a balanced reading program, we have an obligation to honor choice according to needs and interests if we want to grow readers to *choose* to read as the years unfold.

📚 BOOK PASS

Larry visits Elaine Eisen's Grade 4 Classroom

With thanks to Joan O'Callaghan

We are always open to promoting a love of reading with students. The Book Pass strategy successfully inspires independent leisure reading and is a fun way to help readers choose books that best suit their interests, needs, and tastes. The activity gives students responsibility for making their own choices. Book Pass allows teachers to find the right book for the right reader. It ignites an authentic, independent reading component of a novel program. Students are happy because they are given a choice. Following the activity, the class becomes a community of independent readers over a period of two to three weeks, as students share their enthusiasms and responses (e.g., in literature circles, response journals, story maps, perspective writing).

To help promote community and help students make text-to-text connections, the offered books should have something in common (e.g., theme, genre). I arrived in Elaine's classroom with a wagonload of novels acquired from my own book collection. For purposes of this visit, the three piles of books had two simple connections: each of the books was a hardcover; and each of the books had been published within the past two years. There was a spread of genres that included science fiction, humor, realistic fiction, mystery, and historical fiction. Some books had less than 200 pages; some more than 300.

The following outlines the procedures used for Book Pass:

1. Books are randomly distributed to students, who are instructed to read the book they have received for three minutes. If a book "grabs" a student, they can opt out of the rotation, or Book Pass, and continue to read their book of choice. If the reader doesn't favor the book, it is passed to someone nearby.
2. Students are then given another three minutes to spend with the new book they have received, while others continue with their first choice.
3. The passing of books continues until most students have found a book that they are unwilling to relinquish. To those who haven't been able to spend time with a book of their choice during the pass, a display of the books remains for students to choose from.

After three book passes, each of the 23 students had a book they wanted to continue reading. I left the books behind in the classroom for students to read independently.

Bookshelf: Popular Titles from Book Pass

These were the ten top titles for Book Pass in Elaine Eisen's class.

Barnhill, Kelly. *The Girl Who Drank the Moon*
Baskin, Nora Raleigh. *Nine, Ten: A September 11 Story*
Beasley, Kate. *Gertie's Leap to Greatness*

Brown, Peter. *The Wild Robot*
Creech, Sharon. *Moo*
Patterson, James & Chris Grabenstein. *Word of Mouse*
Pennypacker, Sara. *Pax*
Stratford, Jordan. *The Wollstonecraft Detective Agency: The Case of the Girl in Grey*
Weeks, Sarah & Gita Varadarajan. *Save Me A Seat*
Wolk, Lawren. *Wolf Hollow*

📖 JUST THE BEGINNING

Larry visits Elaine Eisen's Grade 4 Classroom

By focusing on the lead sentence or opening sentences of a novel, readers can learn about the characters, plot, setting, or conflict of the novel. Just from the opening of a novel, many readers can generally make an assumption about whether they are going to enjoy the novel or not. Of course, judgments can be made from the cover of the book, the book's length, a book blurb, or even information that has been shared by friends, a teacher, or a librarian to promote the book. The Just the Beginning reproducible master on page 27 invites readers to consider just the beginning of a book and decide whether they are motivated or not to read on.

Here are some student responses I received:

> The two brothers Genie and Ernie really connect to my life with my sister. Just like the two characters in the novel, we don't get along too well. I play pranks on my sister and she tries to act cool all the time. My sister is like Ernie but I'm not really like Genie, but I guess I'm Genie-ish. Then again, my feet smell bad just like Ernie's feet.
> — Dennis L. on *As Brave As You* by Jason Reynolds

> I'm really liking this book because it is one of those girl-meets-animal stories. Both characters are very interesting and unique. The girl is an albino and the mouse is blue and very intelligent. In *Word Of Mouse*, a mouse gets separated from his family until he meets lots of friends and a generous amount of foes. Whether human or animal, this book is for you!
> — Glen C. on *Word of Mouse* by James Patterson and Chris Grabenstein

> I like *Gertie's Leap to Greatness* because Gertie is just like me and Gertie stays calm no matter what she is going through. I like that she never gives up and I would like to think I'm like that. I am going to keep reading because I want to see how she copes with the seat-stealer. Gertie is a very courageous character. I wonder how strong she will continue to be.
> — Angelina W. on *Gertie's Leap to Greatness* by Kate Beasley

CHAPTER PASS

Larry visits Rachel Stein's Grade 6 Classroom

In January 2017, it was announced that the novel *The Girl Who Drank the Moon* by Kelly Barnhill had just won the Newbery Medal for most distinguished contribution to American literature for children. The following week I was invited into a Grade 6 classroom and decided to introduce the novel to the 27 students, hoping to motivate some into reading the prize-winning book.

In *The Girl Who Drank the Moon* by Kelly Barnhill, Xan is a kind witch who lives in the forest of Protectorate and delivers the infants left with her to loving families. Xan accidentally feeds a baby moonlight instead of starlight, thus nourishing the child with extraordinary magic. Xan knows that she must raise the girl, named Luna, as her own. As she approaches the age of thirteen, Luna's magic is strengthened. A Swamp Monster named Glerk, a perfectly Tiny Dragon named Fyrian, and a plotting citizen who is determined to kill the witch all play a part in this powerful fantasy adventure.

There are 48 chapters in the novel. Each chapter is introduced by a sentence fragment: e.g., *Chapter 1: In Which A Story is Told; Chapter 2, In Which an Unfortunate Woman Goes Quite Mad; Chapter 3. In Which a Witch Accidentally Enmagics an Infant.* The chapter titles serve to summarize the plot events of that chapter, raise questions, and inspire predictions about what might take place in that chapter.

Lesson Outline

1. I had photocopied the first page of each of the chapters. I randomly distributed a single page to each student.
2. Students read their passages independently. They then responded by completing two sentence stems:

    > By reading this excerpted text, I learned…
    > I wondered about…

3. Students met in pairs to share their responses. Many students attempted to make connections using information they had learned. Partners brainstormed questions they had wondered about the story.
4. I entered in role as the girl in the story. Students, as villagers, asked me questions. Having read the story, I could supply factual information from Barnhill's narrative; in role, I was able to invent some details that would answer the questions.
5. As a final activity, students met in groups of four to share information from the written text and from the in-role interview, and to discuss the story.

Before leaving, I asked, "How many think that they would like to read this novel?" Out of 27 students, 18 hands were raised. I delivered five copies of the novel to the class in the following week.

Just the Beginning

My father lead the way through the dark, my mother behind him, my sister in her arms, and I was just behind them.

— from *Walking Home* by Eric Walters

After reading this opening or lead sentence from the novel you learn three things: the story's characters (family of four); a hint of the setting (dark); and the voice the novel is told from (first person). In your head a story is beginning to emerge as you visualize the scene, raise questions about what is happening, and make predictions about what might happen.

Select a novel to read. Write the first sentence of the novel. Some lead sentences are short. For this activity you can focus on the first one to three sentences, if that is more suitable.

Meet with a partner who has chosen a different novel. The following questions will guide a discussion about the lead sentence of the novel.

PART A: Paired Discussion

1. What information do you learn from the lead sentence?
2. What questions do you have about the story?
3. What do you predict might happen as the chapter continues?
4. How does this novel appeal to you as a reader (or not)?

PART B: Independent

1. The lead sentence contains_____ words.
2. The author introduces one or more characters. _____ Yes _____ No
3. The author describes the setting. _____ Yes _____ No
4. The author gives a hint about the conflict in the novel. _____ Yes _____ No
5. The story will be told in the first person, from the point of view of "I." _____ Yes _____ No

List three questions you have about the novel after reading the opening.

1.

2.

3.

Are you looking forward to reading this novel? Why or why not?

Pembroke Publishers ©2017 *Take Me to Your Readers* by Larry Swartz ISBN 978-1-55138-326-2

Lead to Read:
Exercising and Monitoring Student Book Choice

In a class of students with diverse reading abilities, there are no easy solutions in matching books to readers. First, we must know our students. What are their needs, their natures, and their lived experiences? What are their interests? What do they believe about themselves as readers? When we know these things we can begin to connect our students to texts they can grow in.

— Anne Poretta, "How a Book Chooses a Student" in *This is a Great Book!*
by Larry Swartz and Shelley Stagg Peterson

Student participation in the book selection process is invaluable in enhancing their motivation to read and in developing their strong identities as readers, as student opinions of the books they read are valued by children and adults within and beyond school. Participation in the selection process also creates a community of readers within the classroom and within the school, as students make recommendations to peers about books they have read by posting their reviews of the books on a classroom or school blog or bulletin board.

In any classroom there will be many students who look forward to reading time, and some who do not. Many appreciate having time to read what they choose to read, catching up where they left off the previous day with a favorite character or discovering more about a topic of interest. Other students seem to sort listlessly through reading materials, taking up much of their time with a search for something to read. In any designated independent reading program, we can observe students who flip through pages without engaging with the material. They are not realizing the benefits of leisure reading. A more structured approach that involves the following is needed:

1. Making a range of reading materials available for leisure reading
2. Helping students select reading materials
3. Creating an engaging environment for reading
4. Monitoring student reading

Title	Author	Type of Book (Genre)	Date Completed

Reading inventories provide a record of the interests and tastes of reader. They also provide a tool to monitor students' reading interests at different times of the year. Students can self-monitor their reading by keeping a record of the titles they have read and listing the genres associated with these titles using a simple chart like the one in the margin.

Bookshelf: Popular Series for Independent Reading

Transitional Readers (Ages 7–10)

Blabey. Aaron. The Bad Guys

Cleary, Beverly. Ramona
Dadey, Debbie, and Marcia Thornton Jones. The Adventures of the Bailey
    School Kids
McDonald, Megan. Judy Moody
Hale, Shannon. The Princess Academy (Also: Princess in Black)
Korman, Gordon. Danger series (trilogy; Also Dive, Everest, Island, Kidnapped
    trilogies)
Martin, Ann M. The Baby-Sitters Club
Osborne, Mary Pope. The Magic Tree House
Pilkey, Dav. Captain Underpants (Also Dog Man)
Scieszka, Jon. The Time Warp Trio
Snicket, Lemony. A Series of Unfortunate Events
Stilton, Geronimo. Geronimo Stilton
Wishinsky, Frieda. Canadian Flyer Adventures

Developing Readers (Ages 9–12)

Applegate, K.A. Animorphs
Colfer, Eoin. Artemis Fowl
Hunter, Erin. Warriors
Kinney, Jeff. Diary of a Wimpy Kid
Lincoln, Peirce. Big Nate
Patterson, James (and others). The Middle Years
Patterson, James and Chris Grabenstein. I Funny
— Treasure Hunters
Riordan, Rick. Percy Jackson and the Olympians
— The Heroes of Olympus
— The Kane Chronicles
Rowling, J. K. Harry Potter
Russell, Rachel Renee. Dork Diaries

Series for Young Adults (Ages 12+)

Aveyard, Victoria. Red Queen
Collins, Suzanne. The Hunger Games
Dashner, James. The Maze Runner
— The Mortality Doctrine
Lore, Pittacus. I Am Number Four
MacHale, D.J. Pendragon
Nix, Garth. Sabriel (trilogy)
Paolini, Christopher. The Inheritance (quadrilogy)
Riggs, Ransom. Miss Peregrine's Peculiar Children
Roth, Veronica. Divergent
Sage, Angie. Septimus Heap
Stewart, Paul and Chris Riddel. The Edge Chronicles

THE TEN-NOVEL PROJECT

Larry's Class

I was concerned that students in my Grade 5 classroom were not making the most of leisure reading time. I observed that many were not sticking with a book once they started. Much of our independent/leisure reading time was being spent choosing books.

I discussed with a colleague how to make the most of the independent reading initiative. We invented the Ten Novel Project. Students were given one week to gather together ten novels they hoped to complete by year's end, three months away. Each student was given a shoe box to decorate and use to store their book choices. If a student decided to stop reading a book, they needed to replace it with another title.

The project required monitoring for student accountability and for assessment purposes. A one page Independent Reading Profile was required for each completed novel; see page 31.

The Ten Novel Project was successful for many students, but not for all. Some students wanted to read books outside the realm of fiction. I accepted that ten novels might have been too ambitious for some who required more time to read novels. Some didn't choose their novels well and needed more guidance and support in selecting books appropriate to their skills. The project did, however, initiate choice according to interest; it did give a focus and structure to the independent program. Perhaps a longer period of time to achieve the goal of ten books, perhaps more teacher intervention, perhaps a broadening of types of text would make this project better for all.

Independent Reading Profile

Title of Book _____

Author _____

Number of Pages _____

1. a) When did you start reading the novel?
    b) When did you finish reading the novel?

2. On a scale from 1 (lowest) to 10 (highest), how would you rate this novel?

    1   2   3   4   5   6   7   8   9   10

Explain your rating.

3. Summarize the novel in exactly 25 words

4. Find a sentence or paragraph from this novel that you particularly liked. Briefly explain your choice.

5. What about his novel reminded you of relations or events in your own life (or the life of someone you know)?

6. If you had the chance, what are three questions that you would ask the author?

    Question 1:

    Question 2:

    Question 3:

7. What did you learn by reading this novel?

8. How did this book help you grow as a reader?

Who Wrote That?
Celebrating an Author through Close Study and Response

An author unit involves the close study of a number of texts by one author. A collection of a specific author's work is experienced, discussed, and written about. In addition, students learn about the interests, experiences, intentions, and style of the author and can gain an awareness and appreciation of the author as a person.

In the primary classroom, teachers can choose to collect picture books by a single author and/or illustrator and share these over time. The picture books can be shared with the community as a read-aloud and can then be made available for students to read in pairs or small groups, independently, or at home shared with families. For a novel investigation of a single author, the teacher may want to read aloud one book as a community read or organize students to read a book by an author using the Literature Circle format. If a large number of titles are available (e.g., authored by Beverly Cleary, Gary Paulsen, Eric Walters), students might make independent choices among them.

The teacher, alone or with students, can

- make a book display of the author's work in the classroom
- use the Internet to gather information about the author
- display biographical information, reviews, articles, posters, and suitable artifacts to help celebrate an author
- collect films, tapes, and YouTube clips of the author's work
- prepare an annotated bibliography of the author's work

📚 AUTHOR STUDY

Guest Voice: Tessa Hoult, Teacher Candidate, Grade 2

A class field trip to see Young People's Theatre production of *Seussical the Musical* provided the impetus for an author study in the Grade 1/2 classroom I was teaching with Mrs. Pringle on my four-week practicum placement. In preparation for the excursion, I chose to read aloud a number of Dr. Seuss titles over a two-week period. As a class, we entered the world of Seuss, a colorful, eccentric world that made us laugh and think, that challenged us as individuals and ultimately brought us together.

Throughout the unit we focused on identifying elements that characterize Dr. Seuss's writing style and narrative, such as rhyming and repetition; the creation of imaginary animals, plants, places, and things; a talent for inventive vocabulary. As the unit unfolded, we also focused on character analysis, identifying character traits and qualities for the characters featured in the stories, and finding evidence to support our descriptions based on the behaviors of the characters. In addition, we identified the larger moral or lesson present in each of the Dr. Seuss stories and its relevance and possible application in our own lives.

Class discussion during and following the stories easily invited critical thinking, debate and exploration of profound and sometimes challenging social justice ideas. For example, *The Lorax* offered an opportunity for analysis of sustainability,

Books featured in *Seussical the Musical*:
Horton Hears a Who
Cat in the Hat
Yertle the Turtle
Green Eggs and Ham
Horton Hatches the Egg
I Had Trouble in Getting to Solla Sollew
The Lorax
McElligot's Pool
If I Ran the Circus
Oh, the Thinks You Can Think
One Fish Two Fish Red Fish Blue Fish
Gertrude McFuzz

Dr. Seuss wrote *Green Eggs and Ham* in response to a challenge, using only 50 different words; *The Cat in the Hat* uses only words from a first-grade vocabulary list. Dr. Seuss theorized that putting such constraints on ourselves actually enhances productivity and forces us to reach our creative potential as we find ways to be successful despite our limitations.

an appreciation and respect for the environment, and the need to take personal responsibility to initiate change. The adventures and behaviors of the characters in Seuss's fictional world often related to real-life connections for many children.

The consistent use of rhyme, repetition, and inventive vocabulary, along with the animated cartoon-like illustrations, made Dr. Seuss easily recognizable. Students became familiar and comfortable with Dr. Seuss's writing style and began to independently recognize and identify literary techniques. In addition, Seuss's rhyming patterns, repetition, and limited word use encouraged phonological awareness and language development. Familiarity not only helped students listen to the stories with enthusiasm and confidence but encouraged them to make text-to-text connections from story to story.

In his unique style, Dr. Seuss uses many unconventional words requiring the use of phonological understanding. Students are often challenged to use existing knowledge of English language conventions to sound out unfamiliar and even made-up words, furthering their language skills. Occasionally I intentionally made miscues or sounded out and reread words while reading one of the stories to the class to remind students that teachers make mistakes too and need to sound out new words just as they do—we are all lifelong learners! The students saw that making mistakes is a necessary part of the learning process and recognized the importance of perseverance in confronting challenges in reading and in life in general. Finally, Dr. Seuss successfully uses humor to capture the attention of his audience. Students were captivated by the silliness of his pictures, characters, and rhyming words. It is through this silliness that students gave themselves permission to express some eccentricity with their own ideas. It was rewarding to witness the potential that students have when they are not only allowed, but encouraged, to think outside of the box.

While there are many subjects, themes, and lessons that can be explored as one familiarizes oneself with the books of Dr. Seuss, we chose to focus on character analysis. Following each story, we would engage in a whole class discussion surrounding the main character. We would develop a list of character traits/qualities, encouraging students to expand their vocabulary and use new descriptor words. The students were also required to find evidence in the story that supported the character trait. In addition, we would compare the characters, and the similarities and differences between them. We could then extend the discussion and make predictions about how each of the characters might behave in a certain situation. While the culminating task to create an advertising poster for *Seussical the Musical* was enjoyable and encouraged the students to think about media literacy and the themes of Dr. Seuss, I believe the character analysis proved most valuable to student learning. In particular, the character analysis of *The Cat in the Hat* led to a valuable lesson that extended beyond literacy.

When analyzing *The Cat in the Hat*, the class claimed that, while the character did many bad things, he didn't "exactly mean to cause trouble, he was just trying to have fun," and then he "helped clean up after and felt sorry and did something good again." The Cat in the Hat could not be neatly categorized according to their usual schema of bad vs. good. This led to further discussion about intentions and higher-order questions, such as *When we do something unintentionally that hurts someone else, are we still wrong?* We concluded that while sometimes the Cat in the Hat behaved selfishly and could be manipulative and bad, everyone has their faults and what was important was that he recognized his mistakes and tried to fix them. Students engaged in the discussion, and also applied what they learned by gaining a better understanding of themselves and others as more complete individuals, encompassing both good and bad. Later, when describing their own behavior or that of others, students would often refer to Seuss characters, making comments such as, "I was trying to be like Horton and keep going even when no one believed me" or "I didn't mean to hurt them but I was being silly and it happened. Kind of like the Cat in the Hat."

Lessons Across the Curriculum

1. *Chart* to compare two Dr. Seuss titles (setting, plot, character, language etc.)
2. *Venn Diagram* to compare the books with the theatre production
3. *Writing* narratives using characters from the Dr. Seuss books
4. *Media: Poster Design* to advertise the play: helped students to consider layout and to capture an audience's attention; also encouraged students to determine an important idea from one of the books and/or to synthesize ideas from more than one book.
5. *YouTube videos and films* to compare verbal text with animation
6. *Vocabulary and Spelling* e.g., highlighting rhyming word pairs
7. *Music*: singing songs from the musical
8. *Dramatization* of one of the stories in small groups

Throughout the Dr. Seuss unit, children often chose to reread the books we had experienced together during independent reading time. They would cheer when it was time to read the new Dr. Seuss book for that day. Enthusiasm spread: they were eager to borrow Seuss books from the school library; many brought in their own Dr. Seuss books from home because they wanted to share them with the rest of the class. I believe that it is through this in-depth exploration of an author's writing style, themes, characters, settings, and created world that a love for reading was inspired in students. When reading with Seuss, children are allowed to laugh and be silly, they are allowed to let their imaginations wander, they are not afraid to make mistakes and take risks; thus they gain confidence in themselves as readers, furthering their love for reading. I was impressed to discover how the children became immersed in the characters and applied their learning to their lives beyond the classroom. Having these characters to relate to and identify with, the children were able to better understand their own behavior and actions as well as those of their peers. This development of empathy seemed to transcend the classroom. As the stories widened their horizons and increased their exposure to a variety of experiences, children were able to apply this newfound knowledge to their own lives. And therein lies the true value of author studies and the immeasurable power of books.

> The more that you READ,
> The more things you will KNOW.
> The more that you LEARN,
> The more places you'll GO.
> —Dr. Seuss, *I Can Read with My Eyes Shut*

And the Winner Is...: When Readers Judge Books

To help students become critical readers, activities are often needed that encourage a close-up look at book or a genre. When students are given opportunities to share their opinions with others, to agree or disagree with the opinions of others, and to consider criteria for what makes a book significant, they can learn to be thoughtful, critical readers. The Picture Book Contest provides a context for students to make judgments as book jurors and to take on the role of those who award monetary prizes and awards in the literary world. Though not officially a contest (there is no prize), this activity can be implemented over several days or can be a week-long activity in which students assess picture books connected by theme, topic, genre, or format. The Picture Book Contest invites students to

- share their opinions with others
- persuade others
- be critical of texts
- consider criteria for what makes a picture book appealing
- read, write, and talk about a picture book
- read independently, in pairs, in small groups, and with the whole class

Annual book awards include
Caldecott Medal
Newbery Medal
Marilyn Baillie (best Canadian Picture Book prize)
Forest of Reading (see page 37)

📚 THE PICTURE BOOK CONTEST

Larry's Class

This outline provides a structure for students to use to respond to books through talk and writing as they work alone, in small groups, and with the whole class. Picture books on a range of topics can be used for this activity; however, to help students better make text-to-text connections, focus on a single issue (e.g., bullying), genre (e.g. nonfiction texts), format (e.g., wordless books), or curriculum study (e.g., animals). In my Grade 2/3 classroom, we looked at humorous books, since I launched the year with an integrated unit on humor that included jokes and riddles, funny poems, comics and graphic stories, picture books and novels.

There is a certain competitive spirit among many students, motivating them to become avid readers. A desire to surpass their peers creates a ripple effect. Students of all reading tastes and levels read voraciously in a variety of genres that they would normally bypass.
— Karen Upper in *Caught In the Middle* by David Booth

Bookshelf: Books that Tickle the Funnybone

Barnett, Mac; illus. Brian Biggs. *Noisy Night*
Daywalt, Drew; illus. Oliver Jeffers. *The Day the Crayons Quit*
Klassen, Jon. *I Want My Hat Back* (trilogy)
Litwin, Eric; illus. James Dean. *Pete the Cat* (series)
Maclear, Kyo; illus. Isabelle Arsenault. *Spork*
novak, b.j. *The Book With No Pictures*
Petty Dev; illus. Mike Boldt. *I Don't Want to Be a Frog*
Pham, LeUyen. *The Bear Who Wasn't There*
Rosenthal, Amy Krouse; illus. Tom Lichtenheld. *Duck! Rabbit!*
Rubin, Adam; illus. Daniel Salmieri. *Dragons Love Tacos* (Sequel: *Dragons Love Tacos 2*)

Stanton, Beck and Matt. *This is a Ball*
Watt, Mélanie. *Scaredy Squirrel* (series)
Willems, Mo. *We Are In a Book* (Elephant and Piggie series)

Phase One

- Reading independently and telling about our choices
- Alone and with a partner

1. Display a range of picture books in the classroom. Invite students to choose a picture book that interests them. Remind them that, if they don't get their first choice of book at this time, the books will be available to be read in the future.
2. Students read the books independently, then write a response. Two focus questions as prompts:

   What might you tell others about this story?
   What is your opinion of this book?

   Alternatively, students can complete A Close Up Look at a Picture Book on page 40.
3. Students work with a partner, telling each other about the book they have read. Pairs choose which of the two books they think would most appeal to others in the class. The book not chosen is returned to the display.

Phase Two

- Considering criteria for judging a book
- Small-group (four students)

1. Two pairs of students match up so that they are working in a group of four. Each pair talks about their book choice.
2. Each group of four decides which of the two books they think would most appeal to others in the class. The other book is returned to the book display.
3. The group of four brainstorms a list of criteria to consider for the rating of the book.

Phase Three (optional)

- Literature Circle discussion
- Small-group (four students)

1. Choose one of the books that has not been chosen as a finalist to read aloud and use to model a Literature Circle discussion.
2. Groups exchange books. Students work in their groups for a Literature Circle discussion about the new book they've received. Volunteers can read the book aloud. The group of four can then discuss why they think this is a good example of a picture book, or not.

Phase Four

- Teacher-led response
- Whole-class

By this stage, there should be four to six finalists, picture books chosen to be displayed in the classroom. Over the course of a week, one book is chosen to be read aloud each day.
- By the end of the week, the class makes a decision about which book is their favorite. Remind students of the criteria used to judge a picture book to help frame their criticisms.
- On the final day, rate the books Gold, Silver, and Bronze winners.

These were the finalists in our class:
Parts by Tedd Arnold
The Dumb Bunnies by Sue Denim (pseudonym for Dav Pilkey) *
Bark, George by Jules Feiffer
The True Story of the Three Little Pigs by Jon Sciezka; Illus. Lane Smith
A Bad Case of Stripes by David Shannon
*class favorite

Phase Five

Extensions

- Responding to a picture book
- Independently, in pairs, small-group, whole-class

The picture book winner can be used as a source for further talk, reading, writing, and/or art activities. For example students can write a review of the book (or other books in the contest) to share with others in the school or community, perhaps on a classroom blog; investigate other books by the author/illustrator as read-aloud selections over a week; prepare a Readers Theatre presentation; create an additional illustration that might have been included in the book, perhaps imitating the style of the illustrator; write a sequel to the book.

See the Forest of Reading website for a full list of current nominees and past winners: http://www.accessola.com/forest/

The Forest of Reading

The Forest of Reading program run by the Ontario Library Association (OLA) has become a successful venture that invigorates reading across Canada. The underlying philosophy of the initiative, first established in 1994, is to encourage, promote, and support Canadian books for readers, which it most certainly does. Moreover, Forest of Reading provides teachers, teacher-librarians, library staff, and parents with a meaningful tool for improving literacy in schools and libraries. Forest of Reading has become the largest recreational reading program in Canada. The unique feature of the program is that students are allowed to make their own choices about reading by voting for their favorite books. It is made up of different categories, named for trees, geared toward readers in Kindergarten to Grade 12, English and French, that include nonfiction and fiction categories. By reading five titles in a given category, students are given the opportunity to determine a winning author. Nominated books for any category are first read, scrutinized, and discussed by a team of volunteer adult readers. These pre-selected lists are made available to students, usually within the school library. Many teachers comment how reluctant readers are excited to select books from the competitive list and often seek out more books by an author or on a similar theme, thus inviting students to deeper into the forest.

INTO THE FOREST OF READING

Guest Voice: Fatma Faraj, Teacher-Librarian

My readers have always gravitated to books with shiny stickers on the front. When asked, their unanimous answer has been that a sticker on the front means it's a good book because it has won an award. When given the opportunity to award a book with a shiny sticker in the Ontario Library Association's annual Forest of Reading event, my readers take their role very seriously. And since the event coincides with the school year, I have realized there are three *R*s of the Forest: the Reveal, the Reading, and the Reward.

The Reveal

The buzz is in the air. The books are about to be announced. Social media is posting, Tweeting, and sharing the news. As a teacher-librarian, I know that sharing the buzz with students helps build excitement around reading. They are aware that a special selection of titles is coming their way. Just as for any movie, TV, or music award, students are hyped to hear the titles. However, once the selections are revealed, it's up to teacher-librarians and teachers to maintain the excitement by reading and promoting the books.

The Reading

Ten books? No problem. The books are purchased, labeled, and stamped. Before handing the books to the student readers, it's important to share them with your school or parent community. I've run the annual event in different ways. As a classroom teacher, I read one of the minimum of five novels aloud to my class. When I ran the Forest in the middle-school library, I invited teachers and members of the school community to be Expert Readers and held lunch-time book club meetings. Now, as an elementary teacher-librarian, I read aloud a Blue Spruce book every week, and introduce the Silver Birch Express and Silver Birch Fiction and Non-Fiction books with book talks. A prominent display is created and the books are introduced to classes, book clubs are formed, and then the books are released to everyone to borrow and read. Wait lists may be long, but the readers are aware they are expected to focus and pass the book to the next person on the list.

The Reward

Yes, you read that correctly—the reward. As a reader, the reward is talking and sharing in a community of readers. The event invites new readers to a club they may not have joined before, as they realize they don't have to like everything they read in this risk-free environment. Most are pleasantly surprised and keep going onto the next book.

As an educator, I've found that this is one of the best lessons in critical literacy, as students discuss—through arguments and agreements—what they liked and didn't like about a book. Readers read a diverse list of books: fiction, nonfiction, graphic novels, picture books, and biographies. It creates opportunities for students to share an opinion and vote on their decision. Some voters share; some voters smile to themselves, vote, and walk away from the ballot box. A young Blue Spruce voter whispered in my colleague's year, "I circled three books because I loved them." Even though her vote didn't count, it goes to show that many books are winners, whether they win the award or not. This year, we gave voters a moment to reflect on how the experience makes a difference with their reading. Most of my readers agreed that it changed how they read by letting them step out of their comfort zone of the "same books" and introducing them to different authors and formats.

It's a never-ending story. Every year my readers reflect on the previous winners; they sometimes revisit the titles or recommend a book to a friend. The *WINNER* sticker shines and the readers smile with pride as they see themselves reflected in the sticker. I may not have a garden to grow flowers, but I am growing a forest of readers, by planting them with books they love to read.

A Close-Up Look at a Picture Book

Your Name _____

Title of Picture Book _____

Author_____ Illustrator _____

Date of publication_____ Publisher _____

1. On a scale of 1 to 10, how would you rate this picture book. Explain.

2. Is the verbal text as strong as the art?   ☐ Yes
                                                                            ☐ No

    Are the illustrations as strong as the verbal text?   ☐ Yes
                                                                            ☐ No

    Is there a balance of information between verbal text and art?   ☐ Yes
                                                                            ☐ No

3. Which illustration(s) had the most impact on you? Explain.

4. What would you tell someone about his picture book?

5. Who do you think would be interested in reading this picture book. Why?

6. As you read this picture book, what did you wonder about?

7. How appropriate is the title? Can you suggest an alternative?

8. How satisfying is the end of this book? Explain.

9. Summarize the book in exactly 25 words.

10. Draw a picture that you think could be included in this book.

Pembroke Publishers ©2017 *Take Me to Your Readers* by Larry Swartz ISBN 978-1-55138-326-2

All Lit Up:
Competition Ignites Readers to Read, Read, Read

1) The Disney movie Frozen was based on what story by Hans Christian Anderson?
2) Who was late for an important date?

—from the Kids' Lit Question Bank

Kids' Lit Quiz aspires to challenge, engage, reward and extend students' recreational reading. It acknowledges that all types of literature is valued and positively affirmed. Its intention is to promote wide-reading across a range of genres and themes.

—from *Kids' Lit Quiz* brochure

Shout-out to Wayne Mills, a New Zealander who conceived the idea of the Kids' Lit Quiz in 1991 as a means of rewarding and recognizing the importance of reading. Wayne Mills not only creates the questions but also serves as Quiz Master throughout each of the worldwide competitions. He affirms that he never asks a question from a book he hasn't read.

Information about venues, equipment, Quiz structure, scoring, and prizes can be found on the Kids' Lit Quiz website: www.kidslitquiz.com

The Kids' Lit Quiz™ (KLQ) is an international literature competition for students aged 10–13. Regional quizzes are held annually in eight countries (New Zealand, United Kingdom, South Africa, Canada, United States, Australia, China, and Singapore) where students write answers to 100 questions arranged thematically into 10 categories. A World Final is held each summer in a different country (Ontario, Canada, 2017).

📚 PREPARING FOR KIDS' LIT QUIZ

Guest Voice: Zrinka Marin-Delic, Intermediate Teacher

Kids' Lit Quiz is known as the Sport of Reading and, like many sports events, the competitive nature of the program ignites participation and raises enthusiasm from those involved. In our school, as for other athletic teams, we hold tryouts, assign coaches and trainers, and hold weekly practices. Different team combinations based on grades, genders, interests, and expertise are created, and the teams complete questions from practice tests for KLQ from the KLQ website.

The initiative has ignited a surge of interest, particularly from our middle-school division, and especially from those who don't always have a chance to take part in a school team experience. As the Canadian coordinator, Nancy Davidson says, "Giving students who read a place to be with like-minded peers is important at this age of 'fitting in.'" As a coach for competing students, I recognize that the Kids' Lit Quiz program gives students who are bookworms an opportunity to participate in an event like an Olympic Games for readers, just like their more athletic peers. The best part is that students work cooperatively to find the answers, can be competitive, and can show off their enthusiasm and knowledge about books.

Prior to the Heats, held in February, interested students met in my classroom over a lunch period. As we met to prepare, rehearse, and test ourselves, some of the questions seemed irrelevant, but when we participated in the Toronto Heat, the effort was worth it. The emphasis on such themes as doors, machines, and mythology seemed to inspire the students to go broader in their reading habits. A long-lasting benefit of the program was experience gained through teamwork. As we worked toward the regional competition, it was rewarding to see students working collaboratively, acknowledging and respecting the knowledge of their peers. Although a final team of four is often selected to represent a school, we were proud that in 2017 our school was able to send two teams, both of which moved to the Ontario Regional finals.

The following is from a Grade 7 student, Alice, who has participated in the event since Grade 4:

> I was introduced to this program in Grade 4 from my teacher and I have loved it ever since. I love it because although it is super competitive, anyone can be good at. The only thing you need is your passion for reading and I guess you need to have pretty good memory too. Even if you don't know much about one subject, there will be another where you get to shine. I thought this really gets us all to work together because we need each other to succeed. I'm so sad this was my last year, but the experience overall has been so much fun!

The following outlines five ways to use KLQ to activate students' prior knowledge of children's literature, as well as igniting and motivating a love of reading:

1. Have students examine questions from previous years, posted on the KLQ website. Use these questions to test their knowledge.
2. Have students write their own questions to be used to test each their teammates' expertise. Questions can be on specific topics or themes:
   - picture books
   - genre focus (e.g., science fiction, poetry)
   - authors
   - animals in literature
   - topics or themes (e.g., magic, water, toys etc.)
3. Using a spelling-bee format, students can compete by answering pre-written questions about books. Each student in turn is given a question to answer and remains in the competition until they answer incorrectly. This competition can be conducted within a class or between two classes in the school.
4. Students can complete Larry's Lit Quiz; see page 43. Teams can then prepare their own lit quiz of twenty questions and exchange quizzes with other teams.

Larry's Lit Quiz

1. Who illustrated *Where The Wild Things Are?*

2. Name Chris Van Allsburg's most popular picture book featuring a train.

3. Name two of Toad's friends who visit him at Toad Hall.

4. Which animal appears most frequently in books by Anthony Browne?

5. What do Jean Little, Sheree Fitch, and Loris Lesynski have in common?

6. What is the title of the first Harry Potter book?

7. What candy treat delights the children in the Narnia series?

8. Who told us that "there is no frigate like a book"?

9. What does the TD bank, the Governor General, and Trees have in common?

10. In children's literature, what do a caterpillar, a ladybug, and a firefly have in common?

11. Name a picture book that is older than 50 years.

12. Name a free verse novel by Kwami Alexander.

13. What is the name of Ezra Jack Keats' most famous picture-book character?

14. Which Canadian author has written more than 100 titles, including novels and picture books?

15. Who wrote *Charlotte's Web?*

16. Which Michael Morpurgo book was turned into a play and a movie?

17. What is August Pullman's sister's name?

18. Which novel came first: *Peter Pan, Alice in Wonderland,* or *Anne of Green Gables*?

18. Name the sequel to Louis Sachar's book *Holes.*

19. Name an Australian book illustrator who won an Academy Award.

20. Who is Lucy Cousins' most famous picture-book character?

Bonus: Name a children's book you have received as a gift.

Pembroke Publishers ©2017 *Take Me to Your Readers* by Larry Swartz ISBN 978-1-55138-326-2

Parents as Partners:
Connecting Home and School Reading

The full report is available at scholastic.ca/readingreport/

Children learn best when home and school literacy environments work together in partnership. Greater parental involvement in education is one of the strongest factors that promotes a child's successes in school. Most parents are sincerely interested in how they can promote a love of books with their children at any elementary-school age. Parents can be involved in the development of literacy: at the beginning of the year when parents meet teachers, through classroom and school newsletters, through classroom websites and blogs, and through parent–teacher interviews during the year, teachers can support a reading program that supports classroom initiatives and as well as one that encourages independent leisure reading habits in the home.

How can parents help support their children's reading? How does school reading compare to home reading? What books do young people enjoy reading the most? In 2017, Scholastic Canada published their first *Kids and Family Reading Report*™ in order to get a better understanding of the reading behaviors and habits of families from around the world. Statistics are available for each of the main topics:

- The State of Kids and Reading in Canada
- What Canadian Kids & Parents Want in Books
- Reading Aloud
- Reading in Canadian Schools
- Summer Reading

In my early years of teaching, I came across a poster that connected to my personal beliefs of reading. On one side of the poster was an image of a young boy hiding under his bedcovers, holding a flashlight to read a book. On the reverse side was a list of suggestions for encouraging parents to encourage reading with their children. The list in the box is adapted from that poster, which hung in my classroom for several years.

Ten Ways to Lead Your Child To Read, Read, Read

1. Take your child to the library.
2. Read to your child every day.
3. Talk about the books your child is reading.
4. Read to your child every day.
5. Let your child see you reading.
6. Read to your child every day.
7. Provide a quiet time and space for independent reading.
8. Read to your child every day.
9. Give your child choice when reading.
10. Read to your child every day.

B&B: BOOK AND BACKPACK

Guest Voice: Jim Giles, Primary Teacher, Professional Development Convenor for ETFO

A version of this article first appeared in *Voice Magazine*, Elementary Teachers' Federation of Ontario, Spring 2002: 8–13.

One way to promote out-of-school reading in which children share books with their families is a Borrow a Book program. Students take home books in a special bag that contains a comment booklet for parents to respond to the reading. When I first read about this initiative in *Real Books for Real Reading* by Linda Hart-Hewins and Jan Wells, I recognized that it allows young children to see their teacher and their parents partnering on something they all feel is important. I liked the idea of having students becoming actively engaged in the process of reading and writing at home and established a Book and Backpack (B&B) initiative that proved to be successful in that it

- addressed the request from some parents for homework
- built interaction between parent, child, and teacher
- connected classroom and home activity
- promoted a love of reading

The class was organized into nine groups of three students. Each group was assigned a durable backpack that was rotated through the group. Every student took the backpack home once every two weeks. To ensure that each students knew when it was his or her turn, children asked their families which evening might be most suitable for sharing. A list of the nine groups, the students within the groups, and a schedule were posted on the classroom wall to ensure that the routine ran smoothly.

The expectations of B&B was that each student share his or her book with a family member. Also, students were asked to respond to the chosen book in some way: through discourse, writing, drawing, or making. Some students wrote to their classmates about the story; some wrote stories patterned on the book; some created new illustrations to accompany the verbal text, some made constructions; a few even made recordings of the conversation they had with their family members. The expectation was that each of the three students assigned a backpack that day would have something prepared and ready to share with their classmates the next day.

The B&B initiative promoted a sense of ownership and commitment in students. It was a program that required a sense of responsibility for ensuring that materials were taken care of and an expectation that the backpack would be returned on the assigned date. Because students knew they would be sharing their ideas and creative work with one another, they became motivated by the expectations and procedures of B&B.

Of special note: Sharing time was crucial to the program's success. Time was set aside each day in class for students to report their involvement in the program. This was an important ritual, and the consistency of routines contributed to success. Students would talk enthusiastically about their book responses and creative work. This show-and-tell promoted language opportunities as students described, explained, questioned, and shared their involvement with the books and their sharing of them at home. As audience, students praised each other's efforts and exchanged positive comments, questions, and suggestions. Motivated by their peers' contributions, students would often "hitchhike" on each other's ideas. The program often continued in the classroom with reading or response activities. Several written stories that had been started at home were developed during class time.

B&B offered students a sense of engagement and empowerment, prompting them to make choices—the choice of which books to read and which extensions to share. When a student enjoyed a particular book, he or she might spend time rereading it, reading it aloud to a friend, or investigating other titles by the same author or books on the same topic or theme.

Many families were satisfied that this program was a meaningful liaison between school work and homework. From the involvement of students, the feedback of parents, and the enthusiasm of the classroom, B&B seemed to be homework that worked.

2

Connected by Genre

Each genre of writing follows rules governing the format, the language patterns, and the effect on the reader. Using genre study in the classroom is similar to studying a theme or doing an author study. However, genre study has many other benefits. Instead of focusing on only one concept or on a limited selection of books from one author, students will explore a type of writing, with the intention of coming to understand the medium and the message. Genre reading can be a helpful tool for students to use to explore, compare, describe, and assess types of books and various forms of writing. Understanding the function of a genre can lead students to experiment with their own writing styles and formats.

There are two ways of describing the term *genre*:
- by form: novels, picture books, nonfiction articles, poetry, etc.
- by function: persuasion, explanation, opinion etc.

Genre study can
- Be used as an organizational frame in a literacy program
- Stimulate students to read other books in the same genre or by the same author
- Help students describe, compare, and talk about books
- Build understanding that print structures help students not only to understand what they read, but also to organize their own writing
- Provide a meaningful context for reading and writing

For Your Consideration

- ☐ How might you define genre? By form? By function?
- ☐ How significant is including a balance of genres in your reading program?
- ☐ Are you familiar with the genres that each student in your class favors?
- ☐ How successfully do you discuss with students the characteristics or rules of a particular genre?
- ☐ How successfully does reading a genre support student genre writing in your program?
- ☐ What genre of fiction do you personally favor? Do you share your enthusiasm with the students?

☐ How do you motivate students to read a wide range of novels? Is this important to you?

☐ Which of the following genre forms are a significant part of your program?

picture books	letters
chapter books or novels	YouTube
magazines	films
newspapers	jokes and riddles
poetry	nonfiction articles
anthologies	nonfiction books
publisher anthologies	graphic stories
taped versions of books	scripts
interactive software	biographies
the Internet	

Picture Book as Biography:
Reading and Writing Nonfiction Narratives

When I was an elementary student, I would take weekly trips to the community library, and I have a strong memory of being drawn to the bookshelf of biographies. These titles were bound in bright orange covers, without any illustration to invite me to choose a book. One summer, I was determined to read biographies of Alexander Graham Bell, Thomas Edison, Leonardo da Vinci, and Albert Einstein. As I write this, I realize that my recent summer reading has included three biographies: *You Don't Have to Say You Love Me* by Sherman Alexie, *Birds Art Life* by Kyo Maclear, and *On the Move* by Oliver Sachs.

Research tells us that the majority of reading we do outside of school is nonfiction, and learning about real people appeals to readers young and old as independent reading. Noteworthy too is the fact that real-life stories of people from the past or the present are often sought out by students embarking on research in social studies, science, or the arts. In a balanced reading program, we need to find a place for reading biographies and autobiographies; we need to use them as mentor texts if we want our students to write biographies.

Biographies and autobiographies are a form of nonfiction narrative. Sometimes, our literacy programs invite students to read and write about real people. The people and events are true, but the presentation of the biography and autobiography can take many formats. Biographies can be about historical figures, athletes, celebrities, sports heroes, scientists, politicians, our neighbors, our classmates. Nonfiction narrative can also include stories that we write about ourselves, i.e., autobiographies.

The desire to learn about someone's life by reading biographies and autobiographies has wide appeal for young readers, adolescents, and adults alike. In recent years, there have been many examples of picture books as biographies. If we want our students to write in this—or any—genre, it is crucial to offer them published samples as models of the writing. This is an important way to connect reading and research and writing.

Bookshelf: Picture Book as Biography

Bouchard, David; paintings by Dennis J. Weber. *Proud to be Métis*

Bryan, Ashley. *Freedom Over Me: Eleven Slaves, their Lives and Dreams Brought to Life*

Bryant, Jen; illus. Boris Kulikov. *Six Dots: A Story of Young Louis Braille*

Dupuis, Jenny Kay and Kathy Kacer; illus. Gillian Newland. *I Am Not a Number*

Giovanni, Nikki; illus. Bryan Collier. *Rosa*

Gottesfeld, Jeff; illus. Peter McCarty. *The Tree in the Courtyard: Looking through Anne Frank's Window*

Markel, Michelle; illus. Nancy Carpenter. *Balderdash! John Newbery and the Boisterous Birth of Children's Books*

McCarney, Rosemary. *Every Day is Malala Day*

The Who Was… series published by Grosset and Dunlap provides biographies suitable for readers aged 7–10 that celebrate a wide range of male and female heroes: *Who was Neil Armstrong?*, *Who Was Walt Disney?*, *Who Was Amelia Earhart?*, *Who Was Rosa Parks?*, etc.

Orgill, Roxane; illus Francis Vallejo. *Jazz Day: The Making of a Famous Photograph*

Nelson, Kadir. *Nelson Mandela*

Pinkney, Andrea Davis; illus. Louis Fancher and Steve Johnson. *A Poem for Peter: The Story of Ezra Jack Keats and the Creation of The Snowy Day*

Rappaport, Doreen; illus. Bryan Collier. *Martin's Big Words*

Steptoe, Javaka. *Radiant Child: The Story of Young Artist Jean-Michel Basquiat*

Sweet, Melissa. *Some Writer! The Story of E.B. White*

Warner, Jody Nyasha; illus. Richard Rudnicki. *Viola Desmond Won't Be Budged*

📖 READING AND WRITING BIOGRAPHIES

Guest Voice: Carol Nash, Grade 6 Teacher

The biography unit provided me with the opportunity to provide instruction that promotes students' skills in researching, recounting, and writing in essay format. Moreover, I found that this genre prompted me to integrate my language-arts program in different curriculum areas, including social studies and science. By focusing on nonfiction narrative, I was able to meet a number of curriculum expectations that included gathering information and writing a report, ordering main ideas and supporting details, and grouping them into structured multi-paragraph pieces of writing.

1. Shared a definition of biography with the students. Discussed examples of some biographies that they were familiar with.
2. The picture book *Martin's Big Words* by Doreen Rappaport was read aloud and served as an example of identifying text features of a biography. A picture walk through the book *Some Writer! The Story of E.B. White* by Melissa Sweet demonstrated various verbal and visual modes of presenting information.
2. As a class, we brainstormed some of the features of biography by listing text features that may appear in a biography: illustrations, photographs, timelines, lists, headings, letters, newspaper headlines, etc.
3. An assortment of biographies and autobiographies were displayed in the classroom.
4. Students worked in groups of two or three, each group given a different sample of biography. I provided them with a checklist of text features and students went on a biography hunt, identifying which text features appeared in the text they were assigned.
5. I taught reading strategies, such as questioning, visualizing, making connections, making inferences, and synthesizing ideas, as advance priming for writing biographies.

Contexts for Biography Writing

1. Writing autobiography:
- Early in the year students were challenged to write an autobiography that told others about themselves in exactly 15 words.
- Prompts for writing an "I am…" list poem was provided as a template for students to create their own first-person poems to serve as an autobiographical outline:

I am...   I dream...
I have...   I am talented at...
I like...   etc.
I wish...

A student-written biography entitled *Terry and Us: A Story of Terry Fox* was facilitated by teacher-librarian Milica O'Brien and published in hard cover by Queen Victoria Public School. Each page of text, written by students from Grades 4 to 6, is centred on a characteristic as it applied to Terry Fox (e.g., cooperation, empathy, integrity), with accompanying watercolor illustrations. The book was published in both English and French and translated into the three predominant first languages of the school community: Tibetan, Tamil, and Vietnamese.

2. The Terry Fox Run is an important initiative at our school and in our community. Students attend an assembly and are encouraged to participate in the annual event. To prepare for this, students have access to videos, the Internet, nonfiction books, the novel *Run* by Eric Walters, and a published picture book about Terry Fox created by a group of ELL students at the school. Following the assembly, students are instructed to write a recount of the assembly and a short biography of this Canadian hero.

3. Remembrance Day provided a context for additional biographical writing in the form of a newspaper report. Students worked in pairs to present a short biography of a war hero. Information was presented as a newspaper report.

4. Black History Month provided a context for each of the students to research an African-Canadian hero who is recognized for his or her contributions. The picture book *Viola Desmond Won't Be Budged* by Jody Nyasha Warner served as a model of nonfiction narrative. By listening to this book as a read-aloud, students gained information about a dynamic Canadian heroine and also learned how information about someone's life can be presented in narrative form. Students were then instructed to identify an African-Canadian to research, including sports figures, scientists, authors, and politicians. A checklist and rubric was presented to the students to guide them through their research. Examples of projects included Dionne Brand, author; Elijah McCoy, inventor; Aubrey Drake Graham (Drake), singer.

I consider the biography units to have been successful based on evidence of progress in students' writing, confidence in speaking, and comprehension in reading. By integrating biography writing throughout the year, I become more aware of students' ability to gather and present information in a clear format. Moreover, I was impressed with the growth in communication skills when students presented their biographies to others. Ultimately, students were able to demonstrate through their various presentations that a biography is more than a list of basic facts like place of birth, education, work, and relationships of a person's life. It involves how a person's experience of these life events helps to make a significant contribution to a community, to the world.

ALPHABET BIOGRAPHIES

Guest Voice: Stacey Whiler

Alphabet autobiographies integrate many aspects of the language-arts curriculum and leave students with a special memento from their junior-grade years. Students created an alphabet autobiography in an art sketchbook, with each page dedicated to a letter of the alphabet and highlighting a topic that is important to the student's life. Names of people, places, activities, and cherished memories filled the pages of the book. Students exercised prioritizing skills in determining which topics to include in their autobiography, and creativity in naming the pages (which must go from A to Z).

For some entries, specific forms of writing (including poetry, letter writing, procedural writing, and persuasive writing) were explored and consolidated. Throughout the unit, students conferenced with their teacher and improved drafts to create final copies; self-editing and peer-editing skills were taught and rehearsed. Students had the opportunity to decorate their autobiographies with art, photographs, pictures, magazine clippings, and various decorations.

This unit connected different forms of writing and demonstrated the ways in which different forms of writing intersect. It explored the limitless possibilities our words can have when we know how to strategically compile them. Additionally, the autobiography provided a venue for rehearsing and consolidating new skills learned when studying new forms of writing.

This unit was accessible to all students and every student experienced success in completing this unit. The opportunity for differentiated instruction was rich and it was easy to accommodate and modify this unit to meet the diverse needs of all classrooms. Students who were eager and finished quickly could always add more detail to their pages: those who require accommodated tasks could easily work on alternatives, while still feeling a sense of accomplishment.

Finally, this project built a sense of community. Students finished this unit by sharing their projects with each other and opening the door to finding connections with classmates, understanding new perspectives, and learning valuable information that may never have otherwise been explored.

Reading Is Not Just for Books: An Up-close Look at Magazines

Some popular magazines for kids:
Highlights
Cricket (also *Spider, Ask, Muse*)
National Geographic Kids
OWL (also *ChickaDEE*)
Sports Illustrated Kids
Wildlife

What we choose to read depends upon a variable list of factors that are centred on needs and interests. In our classrooms we need to move toward supporting readers' decisions about the print resources they select—newspapers, novels, magazines, instruction manuals. Appreciating literature is a lifelong process that is dependent on personal background, language and thinking skills, life experiences, familiarity with the type of selection, the purpose and payoff for the reading, and the situation in which the reading takes place. When a group of middle-school students was asked, "How do we know someone is a good reader?" the majority answered that it was the number of books someone reads and the size of the books. Good readers seem to be identified by fiction, but as statistics show that many adolescents and adults—mostly males, but not all—choose not to read fiction at all outside the school system.

Magazines are an accessible medium for engaging readers. Because they are centred on a wide range of topics, there is likely something for everyone when it comes to magazines. In the classroom, attention-literacy development can be enriched by using magazines as a focus study that respects interests and develops skills in making meaning from print and visual conventions. Students of all ages might be drawn to magazines in the school and community library, have a personal subscription to a magazine, or peruse them in the bookstore. With magazines, students might not feel burdened to read lengthy text. As students decide which articles and pages they will home in on when reading a magazine, the element of choice is respected. Magazines are a medium for authentic reading, since we choose to read what we want at our leisure, whether it's about sports, fashion, animals, food, science, or celebrity. We can make our classroom a doctor's office where we can be drawn into reading whatever is offered in magazine or journals in the waiting room.

📚 TEXT SCAVENGERS

Guest Voice: Stephanie Cini, Grade 4/5 Teacher

Students often think that, when they are asked to read, they have to pick up a book. Why aren't they as inclined to pick up other types of print? I believe that their choices are highly influenced by what we expose them to. To engage our learners and sustain their interests, we need to allow them access to a variety of print, both online and in hardcopy form. We always have to keep in mind that our audience is made up of diverse learners with varying needs, interests, and curiosities. So how do we sustain the interests of all our readers?

Through inquiry, my students chose to investigate magazines during one of our Media Literacy classes. They wanted to explore the various genres covered, reveal the types of writing forms included, investigate how authors were able to integrate subject areas, and discover how techniques and conventions were used to convey meaning.

1. Genre Hunt

We began by deconstructing magazines, both online and in print, looking at the various writing forms within, such as narratives, recounts, procedures, persuasive pieces, reports, explanations, etc. Students were invited to explore the many genres presented. Students were asked to pair up, look through a magazine of their choosing, and go on a genre hunt to record their findings. I next set up a Padlet account and provided each pair of students with a laptop or tablet. Padlet is an online sticky note board that allows students to collaborate online in real time. Students simply get online and enter the URL provided for the board I wish them to access. They click on the screen and up pops a sticky note. They type in their ideas and simply post. The best part is that all groups get to work on one board at the same time. They can post at their own pace and include as many ideas as they wish. Every time an idea is posted on the board, it pops up for everyone to see. Ideas are collected, shared, and explored.

2. Media Convention Scavenger Hunt

In the next lesson, students were provided with a list of media conventions and techniques. They were challenged to journey through their magazines of choice and indicate on which page they discovered a particular convention and how it conveyed meaning. The scavenger hunt included such conventions as close-ups, camera angles, types of print, backgrounds, illustrations, visual details, use of space, etc. They were encouraged to add to my list along the way. Students were paired up and instructed to use the same magazines as for the first lesson, in hope that they would begin to dig deeper into the media text to understand it more thoroughly. Again, sticky notes were placed on magazine pages to designate the conventions that appeared on each page. Students then recorded their list of conventions on a chart.

3. Considering Audience

The third component was to focus on audience responses, looking at who would possibly like and/or dislike the magazines they chose to investigate. Students were prompted to think about gender, culture, background, education, race, age, occupation, maturity, etc. when justifying their responses.

4. Culminating Task: A Class Magazine

Since students showed such an interest in magazines, we decided as a class to create our own magazines in small groups using Google Slides. Google Slides allows multiple students to work on the same assignment at the same time. Some students created their own Team Drive where they could chat and share information while working on their magazine together. To integrate into other subject areas, students were asked to base their magazine on an inquiry topic investigated during their social studies or science classes. In this way, students were able to make connections between reading, writing, media literacy, social studies, and science and technology. What a great way to show students how learning is not isolated but rather an integrated process! What a great way to emphasize that reading is not just books.

Lifting the Word Off the Page: Reading Poems Aloud

Utterature is all literature that depends upon the human voice and a community of listeners to have a life!

To utter means to "outer," to voice. Poetry is more utterature than literature. A poem can be read in solitude and silence, of course, and a connection is made between the poet and the reader. But the inner ear will still hear the chime in the rhyme, the beat in the feet, the inherent musicality of every word. When poetry is lifted off the page and shared, it connects us to each other.

—Sheree Fitch from *The Poetry Experience*
by Sheree Fitch and Larry Swartz

When poems are read aloud, the heart and core of the poem emerges.

— David Booth and Bill Moore, *Poems Please*

When you read a poem on a page it is nothing but black ink on white paper. When you read the poem aloud, you can animate print, making it come to life through your voice. Like a song, much poetry is meant to be experienced out loud. When teachers read poems to students, they become models of reading behavior in phrasing, rhythm, and nuance, demonstrating how print can hold a richness of meaning. Often a change in voice or pace alters the mood and intent. Reciting or chanting a poem requires more than memorizing the sequence of words. Reading aloud helps to internalize the poet's intent, as the reader(s) become familiar with the flavor of the words, their cadence and flow. Gesture, movement, and involvement can also help illuminate the poem's meaning. For most children, the poems of their lives come from their teachers' voices, and the experience must be a special one to enrich and accelerate their enjoyment and understanding of the poet's art.

When students read aloud, their eyes and ears are exploring the rhythms of language. When done well, oral interpretation can improve comprehension skills, helping students come to grips with all the meaning to which the words give rise. Unrehearsed oral reading can be a troubled time for many students. If a student is going to read aloud for an audience, there should be a legitimate reason for doing so (e.g., sharing favorites, reading their own poems, buddy reading, assigned poem of the day) and time should be given to practice so that the child can think about what she or he is reading.

Involving them in reading a poem aloud in pairs, in a small group or as a whole class, is one of the most effective ways to involve students in the enjoyment of poetry. Choral speaking (also known as choral dramatization, chanting, join-in reading, or orchestrated reading) encourages students to manipulate and play with a text. When poems are read aloud with others, they engage students through the use of repetition, refrain, rhythm, rhyme, and repeated syntactic patterns; the poems may ring in their heads for the rest of their lives. After hearing many poems, students come to know what different kinds of poetry sound like.

In my early years of teaching, I listened to Bill Martin, Jr., speak at a language-arts conference where he demonstrate the joy and power of reading poems aloud. He explained to the audience: "We do this kind of activity with children because they are able to transform what they receive and make it their own."

Also, by seeing and hearing a selection repeatedly, students come to learn by heart the sight and sounds of words.

Ten Ways to Read a Poem Out Loud Chorally

1. **Echo Reading**: Teacher reads a part; students echo the teacher.
2. **Cloze Technique**: At least one word is omitted; groups join in to complete the line.
3. **Alternative reading**: Teacher reads one line; students read the next.
4. **Two Groups**: Class is divided into two groups for alternative reading.
5. **Unison**: Once familiar with poem, students read it together.
6. **Assignment of Lines**: Individuals or groups are assigned parts to read aloud.
7. **Use of Soft and Loud Voices**: Vary the volume; also, vary the tempo.
8. **Rhythm Clapping**: Students clap, tap knees, or finger snap as lines are read aloud.
9. **Singing**: Sometimes a familiar tune can be used to "sing" the poem
10. **As a Round**: Students, in groups, read the whole poem; each group starts (and ends) at a different time.

Bookshelf: Poetry Collections

Alexander, Kwame, with Chris Colderley and Marjory Wentworth. *Out of Wonder: Poems Celebrating Poets* (Also *Animal Ark: Celebrating the Wild World in Poetry and Pictures*)

Booth, David (ed.) *'Til All the Stars Have Fallen* (Also *Images of Nature*)

Booth, David and Larry Swartz (eds.) *The Bully, The Bullied, The Bystander, The Brave*

Florian, Douglas. *Zoo's Who* (Also *Insectlopedia*; *Mammalabilia*)

Florian, Douglas. *Autumnblings* (Also *Summersaults*; *Handsprings*; *Winter Eyes*)

Little, Jean. *I Gave My Mom a Castle* (Also *Hey World, Here I Am!*)

Heidbreder, Robert. *See Saw Saskatchewan* (Also: *Eenie Meenie Manitoba*)

Janeczko, Paul B. *The Place My Words are Looking For*

Kuskin, Karla. *Moon, Have You Met My Mother?*

Prelutsky, Jack. *It's Raining Pigs and Noodles* (Also *The New Kid on the Block*; *A Pizza the Size of the Sun*; *Something Big Has Been Here*)

Scieszka, Jon, *Science Verse*

Silverstein, Shel. *Where the Sidewalk Ends* (Also *Falling Up*; *A Light in the Attic*)

Smith, Charles R. *Rimshots*

Stevenson, James. *Popcorn* (Also *Sweet Corn*; *Cornflakes*; *Candy Corn*)

Weatherford, Carole Boston. *Remember the Bridge: Poems of a People*

Out-Loud Poetry

Angelou, Maya; illus. Jean-Michel Basquiat. *Life Doesn't Frighten Me*

Booth, David (ed.) *Doctor Knickerbocker and Other Rhymes*

Booth, David. *Head to Toe Spaghetti and Other Tasty Poems*

Dunn, Sonja. *All Together Now*

Fitch, Sheree. *If You Could Wear My Sneakers* (Also *There Were Monkeys in the Kitchen*; *I Am Small*; *Sleeping Dragons All Around*; *Toes in My Nose*)

Florian, Douglas. *Laugh-eteria.* (Also *Bing, Bang, Bong*)
Giovanni, Nikki. *Hip Hop Speaks to Children: A Celebration of Poetry with a Beat*
Lee, Dennis. *Bubblegum Delicious* (Also *Alligator Pie; Garbage Delight; The Ice Cream Store; Jelly Belly*)
Lesynski, Loris. *Nothing Beats a Pizza* (Also *Dirty Dog Boogie*)
Marsden, John. *Prayer for the 21st Century*

📚 READING A POEM ALOUD ON MY OWN: SUPPORTING SPECIAL ED STUDENTS IN READING, WRITING, AND LOVING POETRY

Guest Voice: Lara Donsky, Special Education Teacher Grades 3/4/5

For three years I taught the most wonderful and creative group of students in my Home School Program in the northwest end of the Toronto District School Board. In my first year teaching this class, there were 12 students that ranged from Grade 3 to Grade 5 with reading abilities spanning from early Kindergarten to grade level. On our first week together we renamed the class Helping Students Progress (HSP). Then we got busy learning to love reading and writing. Of my students, 10 of the 12 were boys. All were disengaged from reading. I used high-interest/low-vocabulary for guided reading; I had a large assortment of books ranging through science fiction, nonfiction, novels, picture books, magazines, etc. in my classroom. Students also had full access to e-books through the virtual library. I tried to appeal to each child's interest, but was continually getting pushback against independent reading.

Through professional reading, discussions, and support with my Educational Assistant and after attending a workshop session, I recognized a need to be more resourceful with poetry. I had used poetry and rhymes when I had taught Kindergarten, but why had I been lax with poetry in my HSP class, especially since there are so many great poetry anthologies to offer them? I use these books for poems of the week and sharing poetry out loud with students. The students really enjoy the poetry but I was not getting the growth in reading success and independent reading at the rate I hoped to achieve.

One day, while looking through the poetry collection in the school library, I came upon a stack of *Urban Voices,* TDSB poetry anthologies written by TDSB students from K to 12. There were ten years worth of books, and more than one copy for each year. Each book covered a huge range of types of poetry and reading difficulty. What a perfect resource! I was excited to present these to my students and, of course, hoped that they would be as excited as I was.

To begin, I handed out a book to each student along with sticky notes. Each student was asked to look through the book, and each time they found a poem they liked or that seemed interesting they were to put a sticky note on that page. Each and every student was engaged. They were making the choices of poems, and at this stage were given no parameters for their selection. I was able to hold one-on-one talks with each student to help narrow down their choices to choose one poem they felt would be good to share with the rest of the group: e.g., *What interested you about this poem? How did the poet present his or her ideas in an interesting way?* Students put their names on the sticky notes on the page of interest. I

Urban Voices is an initiative in the Toronto District School Board by which students from Grades JK to 8 are invited to submit poetry for publication.

then photocopied the poems, slightly increasing the font of the print. The next task to help the students dig deeper into the poem was to have them read the poem aloud to the rest of the group.

During the first week of the initiative, students were given independent reading time every day to practice their poems. They practiced alone and then with at least two different peers. During the process I audio-recorded the students. They were encouraged to take a copy of the recording home (in their poetry folders) and practice.

The final event was a celebration day, when students presented their poems to their classmates. At the end of the week, each student, somewhat nervous at first, approached the class and read the poem out loud. Performances were recorded on the interactive whiteboard.

The success of this first episode encouraged the students to continue the process throughout the month. We followed the same path: choose a poem; rehearse the poem; read the poem out loud; create a goal. How rewarding it was to see the range of readers grow in their confidence and ability to speak in front of others. I was impressed by the increase of self-esteem and growth of comprehension of my struggling readers in the program. How rewarding it was to witness how poetry indeed Helped Students Progress!

CHORAL DRAMATIZATION

Larry visits Liza Taylor's Grade 3 Classroom

Choral speaking invites students to read aloud such texts as rhymes and poems by assigning parts among group members. By working with peers to read aloud poems on a particular theme or topic, or by a single poet, students take part in a creative activity that involves experimentation with voice, sound, gesture, and movement. Because of these variations, no two oral interpretations of a single poem are alike.

Choral speaking enhances students' skills of reading aloud and presentation. More important, however, is the fact that when students work in small groups to read aloud together, their problem-solving skills are likely to be enriched as they make decisions about the best way to present a poem.

Choral speaking is a structured oral language activity that helped me to teach reading, talk, and drama. The activity uses poems as scripts, and as with scripts, the students need to lift the words from the page through voice and perhaps movement. Inviting students to work in groups to perform a poem provided them with a forum to rehearse a short piece of text and present it to an audience. After exploring a variety of ways to read a poem aloud in a shared reading experience with the whole class, students were arranged in groups of three or four. Each group was given a short poem to read aloud chorally and challenged to read it together in a manner of their choice (see list on page 56). Once the groups rehearsed their presentations and each member was familiar with their part, each small group shared its rhyme performance with other groups.

Choosing Poems	Ways of Working
• Poems by a single poet • Poems on a single theme • Poems from an anthology	• Each group is given the same poem. • Each group is given a different poem. • A longer poem is divided into parts, with each part assigned to a group.

Reprinted with permission from Rubicon Publishing.

For this activity, poems taken from a single anthology were used for exploration. *Head to Toe Spaghetti and Other Tasty Poems* by David Booth serves a collection of poems celebrating a banquet of food to delight readers, inviting them to think about their own food experiences with family and friends.

The following questions guided the students through the process:

- How were the lines divided among group members? Which lines were said by one person? By everyone?
- How did the group begin and end the presentation? Were members standing or sitting. Was there a tableau at the beginning or end?
- What voices were used to interpret the poem out loud? For example, how did using soft or loud voices add meaning to the presentation?
- How was gesture and movement implemented to dramatically enhance the presentation?
- Was each person familiar with his or her part?

A DANGEROUS DRINK

24 cans
No more, no less
Soda-filled
I must confess.

Cola and grape
Lemon and lime,
Cherry and berry,
Soda time!

Flip the cap,
Welcome the hissssssss,
Tilt the can –
A carbonated kisssssssss!

AHHHHHHHHHHHHHH

JELL-O FANATIC

Wiggle and **swiggle**
O what a sight!
A bowlful of pleasure
Jiggle delight

Jell-O for breakfast
Jell-O at noon
Jell-O for dinner
Spoon after spoon.

Dreaming of Jell-O
I lie in my room,
I stare through my window
Night will come soon.

And there on the lake,
A **jiggling** delight,
A round Jell-O moon
Saying good night.

Exploring a Novel Form:
Reading the Free Verse Novel

I am sorry to say
I do not really understand
the tiger tiger burning bright poem
but at least it sounded good
in my ears

—Sharon Creech, *Love That Dog*

Traditionally, we consider novels to be arranged in different chapters. Some books have titled chapters, some are structured into different sections. Since the success of the 1998 Newbery Medal winner *Out of the Dust* by Karen Hesse, many authors of children's literature have expanded the novel form by presenting the story in different formats. Gaining popularity over the past two decades has been the verse novel, usually a series of free-verse poems presented in a sequence that builds the narrative. Each poem is usually no more than two or three pages in length. Free verse novels may be told in the first person (*Love That Dog* by Sharon Creech, *Unbound* by Ann E. Burg), third person (*Booked* by Kwame Alexander), or from the points of view of different characters (*The Crazy Man* by Pamela Porter and *The Gospel Truth* by Caroline Pignat). Though the free verse novel is a popular format for young adults, a number of free verse novels have been written for readers aged 8 through 12.

The appeal of reading free verse novels may be attributed to the following:
- They take a very visual aspect, depending on how the author constructs the verse.
- They give a strong sense of character voice, whether told in first or third person.
- Lines may be one or two words in length, white spaces in between verses; not as much text on the page as a traditional novel.
- They appeal to reluctant readers, because they are less intimidating to look at.
- Each poem seems to end with a punch; something to linger over.
- Strong images are conveyed that appeal to the senses.
- They can be written with no guidelines for construction of lines, as opposed to verse written in a strict style with specific stanza limitations. Sometimes verse rhymes but most often it does not.

Bookshelf: Free Verse Novels

Young Readers

Bauer, Marion Dane. *Little Dog Lost*
Creech, Sharon. *Love that Dog* (Sequel: *Hate that Cat;* Also *Moo*)
Lowry, Lois. *Stay*
Sternberg, Julie; illus. Matthew Cordell. *Like Pickle Juice on a Cookie*
Wissinger, Tamera Will; illus. Matthew Cordell. *Gone Fishing*

Middle Years

Applegate, Katherine. *Home of the Brave*

Burg, Ann E. *All the Broken Pieces* (Also *Unbound*)

Bryant, Jen. *Pieces of Georgia*

Cheng, Andrea. *Where the Steps Were*

Frost, Helen. *Spinning Through the Universe*

Green, Shari. *Root Beer Candy and Other Miracles*

Herrick, Steven. *Naked Bunyip Dancing*

Hilton, Marilyn. *Full Cicada Moon*

Lai, Thanhha. *Inside Out and Back Again*

Pinkney, Andrea Davis. *The Red Pencil*

Porter, Pamela. *The Crazy Man*

Shovan, Laura. *The Last Fifth Grade of Emerson Elementary*

Smith, Hope Anita. *The Way a Door Closes*

Sonnichsen, A.L.; illus. Amy June Bates. *Red Butterfly*

Young Adult

Alexander, Kwame. *The Crossover* (Also *Booked*; *Solo*)

Clark, Kristin Elizabeth. *Freakboy*

Cormier, Robert. *Frenchtown Summer*

Crossan, Sara. *One*

Herrick, Steven. *The Wolf*

Hesse, Karen. *Out of the Dust* (Also *Aleutian Sparrow*)

Holt, K. A. *House Arrest*

Hopkins, Ellen. *Tricks*

Major, Kevin. *Ann and Seamus*

Pignat, Caroline. *The Gospel Truth*

Rylant, Cynthia. *Ludie's Life*

Woodson, Jacqueline. *Brown Girl Dreaming* (Also *Locomotion*; sequel: *Peace, Locomotion*; *After Tupac and D. Foster*)

📚 READING AND RESPONDING TO VERSE NOVELS

Guest Voice: Ernest Agbuya, Grade 7 Teacher

Using the local and community library, finding books from our classroom shelves, and asking colleagues to share titles, I gathered together a collection of thirty novels that were presented in free verse. Connected by format style, the books varied in theme and content. Some books were about the refugee experience; some were about middle-school relationships; some were set in the past; some were auto-biographical; some were funny; some gave a punch to the heart. I believe that the verse novel as a form of storytelling can engage readers with poetry, though some may argue that the format puts imagery and language before character and narrative, important aspects of the "normal" novel. Using free verse novels provided me with the opportunity to engage my students with poetry at the same time as inviting them to examine a particular novel form. Moreover, the unit provided me with a context for integrating reading, writing and talk and the arts.

Ten Events for Reading, Responding and Writing Free Verse Poetry

1. Students were introduced to free verse novels by reading a two page excerpt from the novel *The Gospel Truth* by Caroline Pignat. As a class we shared information that we knew about the character(s) and the situation, what we inferred, and what we predicted might happen.

   Each student was given a different free verse poem from the novel. Students met in groups to share facts that they learned, synthesize information drawn from their excerpts, and make predictions about what they thought was going to happen in the novel.

2. Each student chose to read a free verse novel independently. The banquet of books was presented to students and they were given a choice of titles to spend time with. As the unit continued, time was provided for students to work in groups to share and compare the books they were reading. As the unit continued, students continued to exchange books with their friends and read a variety of verse novels.

3. Students wrote a diary entry from the perspective of a character in their novel. The in-role writing provided students with the opportunity to retell a story from the character's point of view, to reflect on the issues and conflicts in the novel, and to build empathetic understanding by stepping into the shoes of others. The diary entry was transformed into a free verse poem.

4. A demonstration was given of how to transform a prose sentence into free verse style. Using the interactive whiteboard made visible the process of manipulating sentences into a poem. Students created free verse poems derived from sentences that appeared in a traditional prose novel or from their own writing.

5. To explicitly experience the strategy of visualization, students chose a snippet/excerpt from the free verse novel they read, and used this text as a stimulus for art.

6. Students were given the opportunity to respond to free verse poems that were not from a novel. Students worked with partners; each pair was given a poem centred on the issue of bullying. Students worked in groups to rehearse and present a choral dramatization of a free verse bully poem.

7. Students created free verse poems using the blackout poetry method using excerpts from the novel *Wonder* by R.J. Palacio. Each student was given the same excerpt from the novel to complete the blackout poetry activity. Then, each student was assigned a different excerpt chapter from the novel to complete a blackout poem.

From *The Girl Who Drank the Moon* by Kelly Barnhill, p. 165

Blackout Poetry

This activity is ideally done using a newspaper article as a resource. However, short excerpts from fiction or nonfiction texts can be used to create blackout poetry. After reading a text, students use a black marker to black out words that may not be essential for understanding. The words that remain on the page comprise a free verse poem.

Tips:

- Students are encouraged to choose a minimum number of words. Once they have gone through the blackout process, they can review the text once again and continue to eliminate words.
- Students can use the computer to re-write and format the "remaining" words as a free verse poem.

8. For a culminating task, the class created a publication entitled *Wonder: The Free Verse Novel*. Each student was assigned a excerpt from the novel from a different character voice. Students reviewed the information from the excerpt to create a one-page free verse poem. Once completed, the student poems were assembled into a collection.

A Tour of the Galaxy: Via's point of view
By Finnoula O

> August
> the sun
>
> me and Mom and Dad
> planets
>
> family
> and friends
>
> asteroids and comets
> orbiting the Sun
>
> all so very
> different
>
> keeping him
> alive
>
> special

9. A class anthology was created where each student contributed a free verse poem on a topic of his or her choice.
10. Students were given the opportunity to reflect on their experiences reading free verse novels and writing free verse poems. The following questions guided their reflections:

   - How many free verse novels did you read during this unit?
   - Which novel was your favorite. Explain.
   - How is reading a free verse novel different/similar to reading novels in a traditional format?
   - Describe your reading experience with the novel.
   - What would you consider to be appealing about reading free verse novels?

 TRANSFORMING PROSE INTO FREE VERSE POETRY

Larry and Ernest Agbuya, Grade 7 Teacher

The following process outlines a method for transforming prose into poetry. It is best to demonstrate the process with students, inviting individuals to make suggestions for line breaks. Using an interactive whiteboard provides an opportunity for students to witness how lines can be continually manipulated.

1. A sentence (or two) is excerpted from a novel.
2. Students insert line breaks where they think the sentence can be divided, with lines that are usually one, two, or three words in length.
3. Students write the poem as free verse, adding white spaces that represent indentation or breaks between stanzas.

Teacher Tips

- There are many variations to the way a free verse poem can be created from a single sentence. As a beginning, each student can be given the same excerpted sentences to work on. Once completed, students can compare poems to note similarities and differences
- This activity is best done with a computer, where students can easily manipulate text until they are satisfied with a free verse format. Students may also choose to change the font for some words.

Here is an example of the process using a sentence from the novel, *The Night Gardener* by Jonathan Auxier (p. 3):

Steam rose from the soil like a phantom, carrying with it a whisper of autumn smoke that had been lying dormant in the frosty ground

Steam rose / from the soil / like a phantom, carrying with it / a whisper / of autumn smoke/ that had been lying / dormant / in the frosty / ground

Steam rose
   from the soil
   like a phantom
carrying with it
   a *whisper*
of autumn smoke
   that had been lying
     d o r m a n t
   in the frosty

ground

Going Graphic:
Reading and Writing Comics and Graphic Texts

The instructional potential in graphic novels is most evident in the way they motivate readers, scaffold meaning, and adapt easily to a variety of learning situations and settings. Taken individually, any one of these three factors must be enough to make educators sit up and notice, but it's the intersection of these strengths that make the medium a perfect choice to support literacy instruction.

— Terry Thompson, Education Week Blog: *The Book Whisperer*
by Donalyn Miller (August 2011)

A graphic novel is a type of comic book, usually with a lengthy and complex storyline. Like a text-only novel, the graphic novel may deal with a complex plot, varied characters and settings, and various subject matters. Graphic novels deliver a range of genres, from superhero to romance, historical fiction, fantasy, science fiction, and *manga* (the Japanese word for "comic book"). They are closely related to comics in that stories are told with the fusion of sequential picture-frames and written text, but the two genres are distinct. Graphic novels suggest a story that has a beginning, middle, and end, as opposed to an ongoing series with continuing characters. Although the length of graphic novels varies, they are usually longer than comics.

Features of graphic novels:
- Format is easily recognizable by storyboard or comic-book style presentation.
- Story is told through illustrations and dialogue balloons with some narration.
- Multi-genre approaches, including adventure, fantasy, humor, biography

This list first appeared in *This is a Great Book!* by Larry Swartz and Shelley Stagg Peterson (2015, p. 58).

Ten Activities with Graphic Novels

Response activities for graphic novels can be somewhat different than for other types of novels, since responses should invite students to pay attention to the text features inherent in the graphic novel format.

1. **Identify text features of a graphic novel.** Graphic novels combine the elements of narrative, speech, illustration, and images that seem to move on the page into a reading experience that is unique. Students can become familiar with the text features by investigating such terms as *panel, gutter, panel border, word balloons, thought bubbles,* and *caption boxes.*
2. **Illustrate panels that might be added into a page of graphic text.** In this way, the reader is making inferences about what might happen in between scenes. By creating images, the reader is also developing the comprehension strategies of sequencing, visualizing, and making predictions.

---

3. **Dramatize stories.** Graphic stories are ideal for dramatization, since students can become the characters on the page and say the words written in the speech balloons. Students can be challenged to represent the different/scenes panels as closely to the words and images featured. Groups can present a part of the story in sequential order, frame by frame.

4. **Present both the narration and dialogue of a story as Readers Theatre.** Since the focus of Readers Theatre is the interpretation of the words, the use of gestures and props is kept to a minimum. Once students have identified their parts (one or more can be assigned the role of narration), they can rehearse different ways to say the words.

5. **Prepare a script.** Students can transform the dialogue from a scene in a graphic novel into a script for performance. In this way, they can consider different ways in which dialogue can be written.

6. **Go on a font hunt.** A change in font size or the use of color brings different meaning to the story. Invite students to examine a section of a graphic text and list different ways that verbal text has been featured. Students can discuss why they think the text has been represented in this way.

7. **Explore how balloons are used**. Students can list and sketch different ways that speech balloons are used in a graphic novel. Discussion can focus on these questions: What are some different shapes and sizes of speech balloons used by the author? Why do you think the author made different choices?

8. **Retell a graphic story as a group.** One person tells the story and the other group members ask questions to clarify the story. The activity can be done in or out of role. Alternatively, students can sit in a circle, with each group member, in turn, contributing to the storytelling. Encourage students to include many details to describe the sights, sounds, conversations, and events from the novel.

9. **Consider points of view shown in illustrations.** Students can examine different ways the scenes have been illustrated to tell a story and establish and mood by looking for close-up, middle-distance, and long-distance scenes. They can then choose one panel and re-illustrate it from a different viewpoint than the author has chosen.

10. **Transform an excerpt from a novel presented in graphic style into graphic format.** Students will need to make decisions about the narrative captions, word balloons, settings, and points of view to tell the story in graphic detail. Large groups (or the whole class) can work collaboratively to present a graphic text of a novel of choice

Bookshelf: Graphic Novels

Graphic novels are available for all ages, including young readers moving into novels (e.g., *Dog Man* series by Dav Pilkey), middle years (*Smile* by Raina Telgemeier and *El Deafo* by Cece Bell), and young adult readers (e.g., *Secret Path* by Gord Downie and Jeff Lemire, *Persepolis* by Marjane Satrapi, and *American Born Chinese* by Gene Luen Yang). Many graphic novels appear as series books through which students follow the dynamic adventures of familiar characters over time (see list below). Also, many popular titles have been transformed into graphic novels to appeal to a new generation who are engaged with striking visual images on the page, just as on screen (e.g., *The Hardy Boys* by Franklin W. Dixon, *The Time War Trio* by Jon Sciescka, *The Babysitters Club* by Ann M. Martin). Single titles such as *Artimus Fowl* by Eoin Colfer, *Coraline* by Neil Gaiman, and *Monster* by Walter Dean Myers have undergone the metamorphosis into graphic novel format, as have such literary classics as *The Hobbit, A Wrinkle in Time, Frankenstein,* and several Shakespeare plays.

Graphic Novel Series

For further support with graphic texts, check out these titles:
Learning to Read with Graphic Power by David Booth and Larry Swartz
In Graphic Detail by David Booth and Kathleen Gould Lundy
Teaching with Graphic Novels by Shelley Stagg Peterson
Adventures in Graphica: Using Comics and Graphic Novels to Teach Comprehension, 2 –6 by Terry Thompson.

For more by Diana Maliszewski on graphic texts, see "The Benefits of Writing Comics" in *Graphic Novels and Comics in the Classroom: Essays on the Educational Power of Sequential Art* by Carrie Kay Syma and Robert G. Weiner (eds.) (2013, pp. 233–235).

GRAPHIC POWER

Guest Voice: Diana Maliszewski, Teacher-Librarian

Through my role as a teacher-librarian who opens her arms wide to engage students with good books, I have come to recognize the power of the graphic novel. Over the past several years, I have witnessed the engagement and enthusiasm of students when selecting books where words and pictures work in tandem to tell a story. A provincial research project about Boys and Reading confirmed my assumptions that many boys seem to favor this unique literary art form. Though we may tend to recognize that boys enjoy comics and graphic stories more than girls, the research project confirmed that indeed both boys and girls enjoy these books.

I have been eager to share graphic titles with students who come into my library and with the teachers who choose to use graphic novels in their programs. Graphic stories appear in picture-book format, as chapter books, and most commonly as the graphic novel, so they can be read by students across a spectrum of grades. Students who enjoy these books are on their way to reading many graphic books by an author, in a series, or a particular genre.

I have come to learn that graphic titles provide significant connection to reading and writing. A further research initiative prompted me to investigate the following questions: Does the medium of comics encourage reluctant writers? How does writing comics differ from creating other writing? What writing skills can be honed by creating comics? I have come to understand that "writing and creating comics produce similar benefits to reading them" (Maliszewski, 2013, pp. 233–235). Some of these benefits include

- Building comprehension by interpreting words and visuals and relating them to knowledge, experiences, and previously read texts in order to make meaning

The use of a document camera and an interactive whiteboard to project the images as you read to a whole class is recommended so that everyone can see the panels and follow along. It also allows the teacher to explicitly focus on the text features inherent in graphic texts.

- Understanding and applying basic conventions of graphic texts, including captions, speech bubbles, thought bubbles, panels
- Creating and interpreting narrative text, dialogue, and illustration to tell a story
- Using comprehension strategies automatically as they occur simultaneously during the reading of a graphic text

The following three events outline learning through comics and graphic texts.

1. Reading Aloud

Reading aloud a single title from a series can inspire students in a single class (with varied skills at reading development) to choose other books in a series for independent reading.

- I read the first book in the Lunch Lady series of adventure graphic novels by Jarrett J. Krosoczka aloud to a Grade 3/4 class, and the fluent, developing, and struggling readers were eager to read a sequel, independently or with a partner. ELL students were part of this group and also eagerly flocked to graphic novels because, as one student remarked, "This doesn't look like a baby book!"

2. Students Create a Graphic Story in Curriculum Areas

Pixton for Schools is currently a popular online access for comic creation. If available on their Mac or PC computers, students can use Comic Life, a user-friendly resource for creating graphic texts. Also, comic book templates can be created collaboratively on Google Draw and Google Slides.

Graphic stories can be used for a wide range of genres and themes, with fantasy and adventure being the most popular. However, after exploring a topic in science, social studies, or health, for example, students can use the graphic-novel format to report information they have gathered.

- I worked in partnership with a Grade 5 teacher on a project that was designed to have students write and illustrate their own short graphic novels on a topic connected to the curriculum. Students were enthusiastic about reading graphic novels for independent reading and were eager to create their own comic stories. Through this project, students came to recognize how words and images work together to tell a story and disseminate messages. Using technology comic creation tools makes it easier for students to create comics efficiently and without despairing at their imagined lack of artistic talent. The following provides an outline of one student's project:

> As part of the healthy living curriculum studied in class, Norah decided to create her own comic entitled "How To Build Strong Bones." Norah gathered facts from nonfiction texts, such as *Bones* by Steve Jenkins and *Bones* by Seymour Simon, along with research on the Internet. Samples of comics online provided a model for Norah, and other students, to follow. Once research was complete, Norah was challenged to present her ideas in graphic format. She favored the use of Bitstrips for School (no longer available) to create her book about bones to share with others.

3) Graphic Texts and English Language Learners

In graphic novel format, author Mark Zuehlke explores Canadian history through the eyes of the Loxley family. Titles include *The Loxleys and Confederation* and *The Loxleys and the War of 1812.*

When teaching about Canadian Confederation to Grade 8 ESL history class, many of the concepts were sophisticated, abstract, and difficult for my students to understand. The students and I used alternatives to the textbook (e.g., *The Loxleys and Confederation* by Mark Zuehlke) as well as comics from *Kayak Magazine: Canada's History Magazine for Kids. Louis Riel: A comic strip biography* by Chester Brown was also a popular resource used in this unit. Comics helped students learning English to strengthen their understanding of the concepts presented, to increase their vocabulary, and to examine the images to assist with comprehension.

I Think I Can Be Persuaded:
A Genre Approach for Reading and Writing

See Mentor Texts in Professional Resources, page 171.

The books we choose to share with our students often serve as strong examples of good writing—as models, anchors, or mentors to inform student writing. Teaching with mentor texts can encourage students to take a close-up look at the way the author presents ideas or information. Using mentor texts is a way for us to "show, not just tell" our students what makes a particular genre successful. When choosing a piece of children's literature to serve as a mentor text that informs and lifts student writing, it is important to deconstruct the features of the text that make it a successful piece of writing. Identifying and explicitly outlining text features of a mentor text helps students consider criteria that can be applied to their own writing. When we are requiring, for example, that students produce persuasive writing pieces, it is essential that we provide them with appropriate mentor texts to demonstrate how authors have presented ideas. These titles may, in fact, spur young writers to write persuasively on topics and issues inherent in the books.

📚 PICTURE BOOKS AS MENTOR TEXTS

Guest Voice: Adrienne Gear, Literacy Support Teacher K–7

In my role as Literacy Support teacher at my elementary school in Vancouver, BC, I work in classrooms from Grades K–7, supporting students in various areas of literacy—reading, writing, literature circles, poetry, and literacy links to the content areas. Whenever I sit down to plan a unit, the first question I ask myself is *What picture book am I going to use to teach this lesson? This unit? This topic?* Because, from my many years of teaching, one thing I know for certain is that there is a picture book for everything! For me, "best practice" is finding the perfect book to inspire and invite rich conversations, deep thinking, and memorable lessons.

This year, my school has been working on introducing different forms of writing at each grade level, exploring such structures as personal narrative, descriptive reports, and procedural, persuasive, and comparative texts. When a teacher comes to me asking for help to teach a particular form, my answer is always, "Let's find a book!" Gone are the days when the nonfiction section of the library was filled with shelves of heavy, dark-bound sets of encyclopedia. Nonfiction children's literature has soared in popularity as educational trends try to incorporate more nonfiction literature into content areas. Over the past several years, I have built up quite a collection of anchor books for different forms of writing. I like to bring a collection of these books into the classroom and invite students to read them. These picture books not only model both the language and structure of different text forms, but also are often creative and entertaining. I also encourage teachers to read these books aloud to the class and then discuss what they noticed about the writing. This way, what students are reading (or what we are reading to them) can have a direct impact on how and what they write.

For a comprehensive outline of Persuasive Writing see: *Nonfiction Writing Power* by Adrienne Gear, Chapter 6: The Power to Persuade (2014, pp. 94–120).

Dear, Mom,
I would like to tell you that I have been thinking how nice it wood be to have a puppy. Did you knwo that puppys can help make your stres go small? Also puppies are cute and so cute and fun to be. Puppies need to be traind and I'm telling you I'm your guy! I will walk and brush and walk the puppy evry day I promiss. I wil stop playing MineCraft firever. Well I look after the pupy and his name will be Frank. Love, your son, Aluas

---

| **Persuasive Writing at a Glance** |

(from *Nonfiction Writing Power* by Adrienne Gear, 2014, p. 94)
- To give an opinion or point of view
- To justify a position
- To persuade or convince your reader
- To encourage readers to purchase something, participate in a specific activity, or think in a certain way

Persuasive writing is a common structure to introduce in elementary grades. The intent of persuasive writing varies, depending on the topic and purpose, but all share the important purpose of stating a position and justifying it. Being able to express your opinion clearly and give supportive reasons to back it up is an essential "real world" writing skill that students need to develop. Teaching the form of persuasion—the standard five-paragraph essay consisting of an opening paragraph to state your opinion or position, followed by three supporting paragraphs, and a final summarizing paragraph—is relatively straightforward. An additional anchor chart with basic transition words and a few helpful visuals, such as "the sandwich" or "hamburger" model have been used to help students construct their persuasive essays—the "bread" on either end of the writing holds their point of view or opinion; the different "fillings" (lettuce, cheese, tomato) are supportive middle paragraphs—and your students will likely be able to write a decent persuasive essay.

What can be more challenging, however, is teaching the persuasive tone, the voice and language fitting for this form of writing. When students are immersed in texts and stories that model the specific persuasive structure and language, and you use these books to anchor your writing lessons, you will be surprised how quickly students will learn to write with a persuasive voice. Many of these mentor or anchor books inspire some great writing lessons—another example of the reading–writing connection!

The following provides an overview of some of my favorite anchor books for introducing effective persuasive skills and the writing lesson inspired from them.

Persuasive Letters

I Wanna Iguana by Karen Kaufman Orloff

A young boy writes letters to his mother, trying to convince her to let him have a pet iguana. Mom writes back giving reasons why she doesn't want him to have one. The exchange of letters and the arguments of both mom and son are sure to evoke a few smiles, but the important lesson drawn from this book is ensuring you have several good reasons to support your argument.

Writing Extension

Have your students write a letter to their parents asking them for something they really want. This could be a pet, or something such as an extended bedtime, allowance increase, having a sleepover, karate lessons, more screen time, etc.

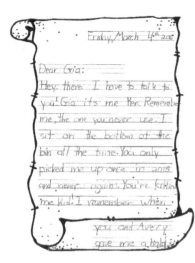

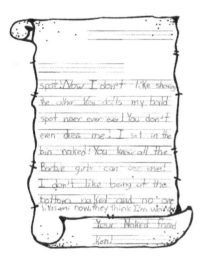

Click, Clack, Moo: Cows That Type by Doreen Cronin and *Dear Mrs. LaRue* by Mark Teague are also excellent choices as anchor books to review the friendly letter format, persuasive techniques, and voice.

Alternatively, they could write to their principal asking for a longer recess or holiday, a four-day school week, or a special guest or activity for the school.

The Day the Crayons Quit by Drew Daywalt

This hilarious, clever book about a box of crayons gone rogue is told in a series of letters from each crayon to Duncan, the owner of the box. Each crayon explains their concerns, frustrations, and a call to action in a very persuasive manner.

Writing Extension

Students think about a toy or item at home that they once loved but, over time, may not have treated very well: they broke it, left it outside, stopped playing with it. In first person, students write letters in the voice of the toy to them, explaining why they are not happy and a possible call to action.

Persuasive Selling

Have I Got a Book for You! by Mélanie Watt

The art of persuasive selling is the subject of this hilarious book by Mélanie Watt. In it, a rather cheesy sales-fox does everything he possibly can to try to sell you the book. Mr. Al Foxward uses many persuasive techniques that make excellent models for having your students write persuasive "book talks" on a favorite book.

Persuasive Causes

Free as the Wind: Saving the Horses on Sable Island by Jamie Bastedo

An important fictionalized account of how, in the 1960s, the wild horses of Sable Island were saved by school children writing letters to the Prime Minister of Canada. This story demonstrates the impact a persuasive voice can be in making a difference.

Writing Extension

This inspiring book is an excellent anchor for a persuasive writing lesson. I like to encourage students to choose an important issue or cause they feel passionate about and write a letter voicing their opinion and recommending a call to action. Ideas can be brainstormed with the class and can include such topics as animals in captivity; a new outdoor swimming pool; the US travel ban; pipeline construction; the sale of pets in pet stores; school uniforms; cell phones in school; payment for good grades; etc. Some of the topics may require research and might need to include current and accurate facts to support the argument.

When you share a picture book to anchor your writing lesson, students will be better able to process a concept, learn text structure, language, and writing tools and techniques. I can't imagine teaching a writing lesson without a picture book in my hand. Best practice, you ask? Find a book!

Bookshelf: Picture Books that Inspire Persuasive Writing

Averbeck, Jim; illus. Yasmeen Ismail. *One Word From Sophia*
Cronin, Doreen; illus. Betsy Lewin. *Click, Clack, Moo! Cows that Type*
Bastedo, James; illus. Susan Tooke. *Free as the Wind: Saving the Horses on Sable Island*
Daywalt, Drew; illus. Oliver Jeffers. *The Day the Crayons Quit*
Orloff, Karen Kaufman; illus. David Catrow. *I Wanna Iguana* (Also *I Wanna New Room)*
Scieszka, Jon; illus. Lane Smith. *The True Story of the Three Little Pigs*
Stinson, Kathy: illus. Robin Baird Lewis. *Red is Best*
Teague, Mark. *Dear Mrs. LaRue: Letters from Obedience School*
Viorst, Judith, *Earrings*
Watt, Mélanie. *Have I Got a Book for You*
Willems, Mo. *Don't Let the Pigeon Drive the Bus*

📚 FROM PICTURE BOOK TO PSA

Guest Voice: Christine Balt, Teacher Candidate

One of the most exciting aspects of being a teacher candidate in Toronto is the chance to engage with diverse school communities. I have had the privilege of learning with and from students from a vast array of cultural and linguistic backgrounds, including those in the process of acquiring English as a spoken and written language. I found myself in a Grade 4 classroom with a rather large percentage of English Language Learners (ELLs) for one of my practicum placements—a unique but nonetheless motivating challenge that led me to seek out appropriate materials to support their learning. I was specifically on the lookout for a picture book that would function as an accessible entry point for the genre of persuasive writing.

A colleague passed on the picture book, *Hey, Little Ant* by Phillip and Hannah Hoose, illustrated by Debbie Tilley, the story of a little ant who is discovered by a large boy. Immediately, the boy wishes to squish the ant with his shoe. Thus begins a battle of the wills in which the boy and the ant use emotional appeal, reasoning, facts, and opinions to argue their respective cases. The boy engages in a range of rhetorical devices to rationalize his need to squish the ant. He says, "But…my mother says that ants are rude. They carry off our picnic food," an example of how stereotypes are exploited to persuade or justify a point of view or action. Similarly, the ant engages in emotional appeal: "One single chip feeds our whole town. You must not let your foot come down."

The language of the book seemed to be accessible to the students without being too simplistic. The use of rhyme and rhythm appealed to students at various levels of English language acquisition. After a whole-class read-aloud, I engaged the students in a reading response activity in which they were asked to apply the methods of persuasion used in the book to create a public service announcement (PSA) convincing the boy to leave the poor ant alone.

With thanks to Fatema Isam

The students were first exposed to PSA examples in both video and poster formats. Then, in groups, students had the choice of creating a short film supported by drama, or a poster consisting of text and an image. The goal was for students to apply the forms of persuasive writing and speech used in *Hey, Little Ant*—emotional appeal, reasoning, facts and opinions—to form a compelling argument to preserve the ant's life. Students were given time in class over a period of a week to create and finalize their PSAs. Upon reflection, I was pleased to see that the ELL learners were integrated into groups as they planned and developed their work. As a final activity, groups were given the opportunity to present their finished products to each other. One group created an effective short dramatic film in which the boy "shrank" in size and met the ant on a more even level. Emotional appeal and reasoning, coupled with the magic of drama, were used to persuade the boy to understand the ant's point of view.

More Than a Play :
When Students Read Scripts Aloud

A theatre script is a particular kind of text, unique because it demands that the words be lifted from the page: they need to be spoken. A good script speaks to us and about us through voice, gesture, stillness, action. In order to find the meaning of the words, we need to empathize with the characters through role-playing and we need to discuss possibilities of speech and action with others. A teacher can work in the role of director and guide students through a palette of strategies to bring meaning to the words on the page, to empower students to find meaning, and to work toward sharing, presenting, and/or performing scripts for an audience.

Some scripts are monologues, meant to be read aloud by one person, but many scripts that we offer students have more than one character. In this way, scripts are a meaningful way to promote collaboration and group participation as students work through animating the print through voice and action.

Titles by Aaron Shepard that are useful resources for exploring Readers Theatre:
Folktales on Stage
Readers on Stage
Stories on Stage

Five Suggestions for Writing and Reading Scripts

1. **Transforming a text selection** into script dialogue involves students in several literacy processes. For example, selecting part of a novel and turning the narrative into dialogue forces careful reading of the text and requires the writer to interpret the prose and maintain the intent of the story and the characters while presenting the thoughts and actions through dialogue.

2. **Graphic novels and/or comics** are yet another text format centred on dialogue. Students can transform a graphic text into a script by including narration, speech balloons, and thought bubbles. Alternatively, transforming a script into a graphic text invites students to inspect the words on the page.

3. **Readers Theatre scripts** are developed from material not initially written for performance. The technique of Readers Theatre allows participants to dramatize narration and dialogue, using selections such as novel excerpts, short stories, or folktales or fables. Readers Theatre does not require participants to memorize a selection; however, before reading the text aloud, group members should think about and discuss the way narration and dialogue can be divided among them.

4. **Scriptwriting** has students creating a short scene in scripted form (recommended to be done in pairs or groups of three or four). The scene could focus on a particular theme or issue, a retelling of a story, or an event that the students have experienced. Writing words that others can then give life to can be challenging. As students write scripts, they are encouraged to read the words aloud often. Pairs or groups can exchange scripts to read aloud. Writers can observe their words being spoken aloud and then both hear and see the need for revision. It is recommended that the students work collaboratively to create a script.

With thanks to colleagues Bob Barton and Debbie Nyman, and to Jim Giles, Elementary Teachers' Federation of Ontario.

5. **Scenes Cont'd** is a strategy in which, after exploring and rehearsing an excerpted scene from a play, students can work collaboratively to write a short script that continues the scene. What might the characters' say next? How will the conflict or dilemma of the scene unfold? Alternatively, students can invent a new scene with the addition of one or more characters.

Bookshelf: Ten Recommended Scripts

Brooks, Martha and Maureen Hunter. *I Met a Bully on the Hill*
Craig, David S. *Danny, King of the Basement*
Foon, Dennis. *New Canadian Kid/Invisible Kids* (Also *Skin*)
Johnson, Marcia. *Binti's Journey*
Levine, Karen and Emil Sher. *Hana's Suitcase on Stage*
Pizano, Beatriz. *La Maleta* (*The Suitcase*)
Roy, Anusree. *Sultans of the Street*
Taylor, Drew Hayden. *Spirit Horse*
Watts, Irene and Robert Munsch; illus. Michael Martchenko. *Munsch at Play: Eight Stage Adaptations for Young Performers* (Also *Munsch at Play: Act Two*)

📚 READING SCRIPTS

Guest Voice: Sheila Jacobs, Grade 7/8 Teacher

A script is a text that demands to be read out loud and is therefore a significant in helping students develop their interpretation skills. I chose to focus on script interpretation in my classroom as it provided me with an opportunity to engage the students with an active, collaborative experience at the same time as providing a meaningful structure to integrate reading and oral communication, as well as an opportunity to integrate literacy and drama.

Working with *More Than A Play* helps students learn about the unique features of a written script, such as character list, stage directions, narrator roles. As students read the scripts aloud and prepare to present and perform them, they experience drama exploration that includes use of voice, rehearsing, revising, gesture, blocking, etc. Moreover, they come to understand the complexities of eliminating intolerance and prejudice in the world. .

Each of the scripts in *More Than A Play* invites students to experience situations from different points of view. Readers become part of the dialogue, rather than just observers. As students bring these scenes to life, they empathize with the characters who are dealing with troubling situations. By stepping into the shoes of others and discussing the issues, students come to understand how these characters might feel. One of my goals in introducing these scripts is to help develop compassionate understanding of real-life situations that connect to script themes.

The addition of scripts to our literacy program allowed students to experience a specific text form up-close. Like short stories, poetry, picture books, and novels, the scripts invited the students to determine important ideas, to infer, to discuss content, to question the text, and to share personal connections, as well as to work with others to uncover and understand universal themes of social justice, diversity, and equity.

More Than A Play is an excellent resource available through the Elementary Teachers' Federation of Ontario (ETFO). The book is a collection of nine short plays written by top Canadian playwrights. The short scripts explore equity and current social-justice issues, such as gender bias, ageism, disability, cyberbullying, racism, and homophobia. The plays in this resource offer stories and themes that demonstrate how young people deal with inequities.

What Are You Watching?
Using Educational TV in the Reading Program

Before becoming a TV series, The Magic School Bus was a series of books by Joanna Cole and Bruce Degen. The stuff of television often explodes into a world of popular culture where clothing, toys, and, yes, books connect young people to what they are watching. *Watch the series/ Read the book*—and vice versa.

Shout-Out:

The Incredible Tales of Weirdwood Manor (created by All Play, No Work) is an interactive reading series available as an app. This fantasy series follows the adventures of three gifted children as they try to uncover the secrets of writer and inventor Arthur Weirdwood and the magical mystical manor in which he resides. Strong 3D graphics, games and puzzles, strange creatures, and a suspenseful plot help to make *Weirdwood Manor* an appealing reading—and viewing— experience.

As young kids—or parents of young kids—the opportunity to watch television, be entertained, and 'learn something' all at the same time has always had wide appeal. How many of us spent hours visiting *Sesame Street, Mister Rogers' Neighborhood,* or *The Backyardigans,* or traveling around the world with *Dora the Explorer, Carmen Sandiego,* or Ms. Frizzle and her Magic School Bus? Many morning or after-school shows remind us that TV isn't all that bad when it comes to education. Sometimes a deliberate attempt to include a series (or part of a series) in our classrooms helps us to give credit to TV screen time, at the same time as providing opportunities to connect media and literacy in our programs. When showing TV shows (or YouTube videos and films), we are providing another text for students to respond to through talk, writing, and the arts. We are giving respect to TV-viewing habits that already motivate many boys and girls, thus connecting our classrooms to school, home, and the outside world.

📖 VIEWING AND RESPONDING TO A TV SERIES

Guest Voice: Jeff Szpirglas, Grade 2 Teacher

Read All About It, for those of you who didn't grow up in Ontario during the early 1980s, was an episodic television series aimed at promoting literacy for young viewers, produced in the heyday of government-funded TV Ontario. It also remains one of the most suspenseful kids shows I've ever seen. I don't say this lightly. *RAAI* stuck with me for thirty-odd years, lumped in a mélange of exciting television series that included *Doctor Who* and *The Greatest American Hero.* You know, the good stuff.

The series centered around the exploits of a trio of plucky kids who inherit an uncle's derelict coach house and turn it into a newspaper. They're investigating a conspiracy in their town of Herbertville, led by a floating alien head called Duneedon (played with menacing gusto by Sean Hewitt). What the show emphasized was the existence of real danger to its young protagonists, who go through weekly adventures, alternatively singing songs about homonyms and being trapped in chambers of toxic gas on alien worlds. Each episode ends on a cliffhanger, and the credits crawl over a freezeframe with unsettling, atonal music. They don't make them like this anymore.

Flash forward many years, and I'm now teaching Grade 2 students, about the same age as I was when I first encountered the show as a kid. Amazingly, the series that had long been forgotten was available on YouTube in highly watchable 480p segments. Would it have the same impact on a generation so far removed from my own childhood? I primed my students, letting them know that we didn't have to commit to the series if they weren't interested, and that, no, it wasn't going to be *too* scary.

I've been screening *RAAI* on a weekly basis to my Grade 2s in the four years since, using the show to promote read-alouds, word-attack skills, and reading strategies, such as connecting and predicting. The show builds in history lessons (the War of

1812), a focus on publishing skills, a breakdown of different poetry genres, and fairy tales. Learning about the newspaper frames the reporting of the adventures in this series, and I know that my understanding of the 5W's of newspaper writing was sparked by this series. *RAAI* provides an opportunity for me to help my students make connections to newspapers and other media they encounter in their own lives.

What amazes me is the magnetic pull this series still has over young audiences. Today's pace of television, not to mention our instantaneous access to it (along with the Internet), has changed the way we engage with media. I keep *RAAI* strictly old-school, screening it one episode at a time, once a week, so there's an excited buildup to the next episode. "What's gonna happen next?" is what drives the series, as a product not to be guzzled, but sipped—despite the fact that some of my students have decided to binge-watch the whole thing in one go.

Given the episodic nature of the show, some of the best activities I've structured are based around making predictions and checking how they turned out as the show progresses. One of the better examples came from a series of episodes in which two protagonists, Lynne and Alex, are sent into the fictitious Book World to help stop the heroes and villains of stories from being erased by the unseen Book Destroyer. For a few weeks, we took the time to guess who or what the Book Destroyer was. Some students thought that the Book Destroyer could have been one of the villains encountered in the narrative, such as Dracula or the Big Bad Wolf, and the final revelation took many students by surprise.

Other groups of my students have created *Read All About It* "movie" posters, and the characters have been woven into a lot of classroom talk. The show has become about as popular in my room as a trip to the computer lab for online activities—no small praise.

Clearly, *Read All About It* is more than just a tradition I've nostalgically revived (although graduates of my Grade 2 class come by to ask what episode I'm screening from time to time). It's a living part of our classroom discussions, informing the content of written morning messages or parts of modeled reading and writing activities. The series is not merely a television relic to be screened by pressing a button, but a springboard for other activities that develop and foster literacy skills I'm actively working on in the classroom.

Teaching literacy through media, even something as old-school as *Read All About It*, highlights that we are working in a multi-literate world, in which pen and paper tasks are no longer the norm (even though, back when *RAAI* was set, they *were*). In an age where information is often instantaneous and overwhelming, it's important to take the time to question what various media are presenting to us, to process and evaluate what is fact and what is fiction. That's all embedded in the story and ideology of *Read All About It*, in which a group of kids are up against a conspiracy that goes right up to their own municipal government.

And what of our learners who are developing literacy skills such as decoding and comprehension? The use of interactive technology and the screening of visual stories, like a television series, provides much-needed visual and auditory cues that still promote strategies that make good readers, such as predicting, questioning, connecting, and evaluating. Wrapping it up in a serialized mystery with horror cliffhangers is just the icing on the cake.

A Note from Larry
I have vivid memory of showing *Read All About It* in my classroom in the 1990s. This was at the same time that Jeff was a young student, watching the series in his elementary classroom. Now Jeff has ensured that *RAAI* is integral to his literacy program. I taught Jeff Szpirglas when he was a teacher candidate in the Initial Teacher Education program more fifteen years ago.

Connected by Response

If books could have more, give more, be more, show more, they would still need readers, who bring to them sound and smell and all the rest that can't be in books.
The book needs you.

—Gary Paulsen, *The Winter Room*

How students respond to what they read can be as important as what they read. Response activities can take the form of discussion, writing, drama, or art. Students can talk about a text, write ideas sparked by the novel, read dialogue aloud, create three-dimensional art, role-play characters and events, illustrate, use the Internet to learn more about a topic, and read other books by the same author, on the same theme or topic, or in the same genre as one they've enjoyed.

Response activities allow readers to open up the text for interpretation and reflection—to make sense of the book they've read. By responding in a format that suits their learning style, students can consider the experience of reading and expand or modify their understanding. Response activities encourage readers to voice viewpoints and opinions and to share and compare these responses with the viewpoints and opinions of others. With careful intervention on the teacher's part, collaborative responses can extend each reader's personal response and help generate a wider and more thoughtful appreciation of the book.

Helping students go beyond the text requires techniques that relate the ideas and concepts in the text to students' experiences and that tap fundamental memories and connections brought forth by the intensity of the reading experience. In the classroom, we can promote and develop students' responses by opening up the text for discussion and encouraging students to reveal and express their ideas and opinions.

The reading of a book is often a complete experience in itself and, as teachers, we need to remind ourselves that we do not always have to ask for an external response from our students. Usually, though, in the context of a literacy program, students should "do something" as a response to what they have read. In this way, students dig deeper into a book's meaning, reveal what is going on inside their heads, and extend their comprehension by collaborating with a partner, small group, or the whole class to find out *Are you thinking what I'm thinking?*

For Your Consideration

- ☐ How often do you provide opportunities for students to express and reflect upon their reading experiences?
- ☐ Are opportunities provided for students to respond to fiction, nonfiction, poetry, media?
- ☐ Is there a balance of talk, writing, and arts-based responses in your literacy program?
- ☐ How much choice do students have in the modes of response?
- ☐ How often do students share their responses with others? With the teacher?
- ☐ How do you respond to student responses?
- ☐ Do your response activities provide opportunities for promoting interpretive, creative, and critical thought?
- ☐ What do book reports mean to you? Do you incorporate alternative response strategies to the book report?
- ☐ What part does technology and/or the Internet play as a medium for response?
- ☐ Do you offer strategies for students to respond to whole-class, small-group, and independent reading?
- ☐ Do you share with students how they will be assessed on their responses?

Not Another Book Report!
Alternative Strategies for Responding to Novels

See *Ban the Book Report* by Graham Foster for more on response activities that encourage, rather than discourage, reading.

I have a rather unpleasant memory of completing book reports during my middle-school years, always with the same format: describe the major characters, describe the minor characters; describe the setting; prepare a plot graph to outline the story events from beginning, through rising action and climax to denouement; and give your opinion of the novel. This was required of us each semester for Grades 7, 8 and 9. The book report did not turn me into a lover of novels; my passion was ignited despite my school literacy experiences, not because of them.

In the early years of my teaching, I relied on what I thought was an appropriate response task. Yes, I found myself assigning book reports on novels students read independently. Then university courses on reading instruction early in my career provided a whack upside my head. I quickly eliminated the traditional book report from my instructional repertoire and challenged myself to find alternative ways to encourage response, ways that engaged students, invited them to dig deeper into the text, and offered opportunities for them to respond in a variety of modes. In fact, I have challenged myself to consider a wide range of instructional strategies that not only engage readers but also lead them to enjoy reading, which is the ultimate goal of this book.

My doctoral thesis (2000) entitled *Text Talk: Towards an Interactive Classroom Model for Encouraging, Supporting and Promoting Literacy* inspired me to conduct research on alternative methods for students to respond to books centred on three assumptions:

1. The Reading Response Journal provides a medium for personal response (drawn from the work of Nancie Atwell). See Response Journals on page 85 for more.
2. Book Talk provides opportunities for students to talk about books in groups and has them interact to share comments, concerns, and criticisms in response to what they have read (drawn from the work of Harvey Daniels). See Literature Circles on page 98 for more.
3. Perspective Writing, in which students "become" characters in the story and write in role as characters from the story, builds empathetic understanding of characters, relationships, and dilemmas (drawn from the work of David Booth and Jonothan Neelands). See Character Journals on page 83 for more.

Reading is personal. The reading of a literary text is, in effect, a dialogue between a reader and a writer, the written text being the vehicle permitting this exchange to occur. The dialogue has the potential for limitless meanings. It was Louise Rosenblatt who brought attention to reading as a transaction process, a kind of conversation between reader and writer, who together shape the ideas captured by the words on the page. Those who recognize reading as a transaction between reader and text see the writer as the one who contributes the words, sentences, and paragraphs to represent his or her views while the reader brings to the text personal experiences, attitudes, thoughts, and feelings. The conversation is not easy: the writer's work is done, and the reader now bears the burden. In his book, *A History of Reading,* Alberto Manguel claims every piece of writing involves a death (the writer) and a life (the reader).

The reader takes considerable responsibility for making meaning —inferring, generalizing, distinguishing fact from opinion, making judgments, visualizing. The reader brings to the text all of their life experiences using the features of the written text: words, paragraphs, conversations, ideas, and imagery. A reader does not become the writer, seeing and thinking as the writer does. Instead the reader shapes the meaning by gathering personal impressions and interpretations.

Six Alternatives to Traditional Book Reports

1. Story Boxes

See page 95 for a detailed description of this strategy.

2. Novel in an Hour

This is a useful activity for having students dig collaboratively into a novel that they have not all read from start to finish. The class is divided into small groups so that each group is responsible for conveying key information from one chapter of the novel. Depending on group size, some chapters can be eliminated from the presentation. After reading its assigned chapter, each group makes a decision about how to depict the chapter's plot and themes. They might choose storytelling in role, Story Theatre, Readers Theatre, tableaux, soundscapes, dance drama, or improvisation. They may want to add props, musical instruments, song, and simple costumes to enhance the dramatic presentation. After preparing and rehearsing, each group, in sequence, presents its chapter to the rest of the class to create the Novel in an Hour. Students should be encouraged to revise and revise their work to create a somewhat polished piece ready to be performed for an audience. Ultimately, the goal is to motivate students to read the novel in its entirety.

3. Book Trailers

Students work independently or in pairs to create a trailer for a novel they have read. A movie trailer takes the important scenes of a full-length movie and weaves them into a coherent and concise idea of what the story is about. A book trailer provides a forum for students to highlight events from a novel with the intention of sparking interest for others to read the novel. For this activity, students need time to prepare images and create their photo stories. Students can act in the trailer as characters from the book, or they can create images or use non-copyright images from the Internet that help tell the story. Even though groups are challenged to create a trailer that is only one minute in length, the activity involves an extended period of time to plan and create their media presentation for an audience. To prepare for this activity, students are encouraged to view website or YouTube book trailers used to promote novels such as *Wonder* by R.J. Palacio, *Flora & Ulysses* by Kate DiCamillo, *Rules* by Cynthia Lord, and *Inside Out and Back Again* by Thanhha Lai. Note: An online class space (Wikispaces or Image Websites) can be created for the links to post book trailers.

An alternative to this is the Novel Pyramid format.

4. 35-Word Novel Study

Students are given a blank sheet of paper. The students fold the sheet from top to bottom three times. When opened the paper will have eight horizontal sections. Using the top section to identify the book, students respond to the book in the rest of the sections according to sentence prompts that provide an opportunity to distil what they think of a novel into 35 words. See 35-Word Novel Summary template on page 87.

Students use their notes to discuss the book they have read with at least one other person who has read a different novel. Students are encouraged to elaborate on each of the items.

5. 100-Word Book Blurb

100 Words provides an opportunity for students to summarize the novel they have read, this time by creating a synopsis or book blurb that tells others about the novel. One purpose of the book synopsis is to interest others in the book, to persuade them to read it, so there needs to be a balance between highlighting the plot and problems of the novel and not giving too much away. When preparing a novel synopsis, the writer needs to

- Summarize the plot
- Explain the major conflict
- Describe the characters and their relationships to one another
- Highlight the main theme(s) of the novel

Direct students to prepare a synopsis of the novel by writing a summary that is exactly 100 words. Doing so means that students will continue to revise and edit, and to endeavor to choose the best words possible to inform others about the novel.

Extensions

- Once book blurbs are completed, students work with a partner who has written a synopsis for the same novel. Partners compare ideas and then combine them to create a new 100-Word summary.
- Challenge students to revise what they have written by putting a 50-word restriction on the book blurb.
- Students can post their book blurb synopses on a class website to inform and invite others to read the recommended books.

6. Text-Message Conversations

This activity affords students an opportunity to focus on character and plot while drawing on technology and media literacy to make inferences. Students select an important or pivotal event or moment in the novel and create an imaginary text-message conversation between two characters from the novel. The conversation might describe or comment on the significant event.

CHARACTER JOURNALS

Larry's Class

The activity described here provides a viable—indeed the best—alternative to the traditional book report. For more than twenty years instructing teacher candidates, I have offered the following assignment in the literacy course, and the results from the more than one thousand teachers who have completed this assignment absolutely shine. Hopefully, this carried forward into classroom practice, since I have found that novel readers of all ages have enjoyed pretending to be a character and inventing and revealing a character's thoughts on paper.

Writing a journal entry from a character's perspective enables each reader to have a conversation with the text, giving the reader as much responsibility as the author in the making of meaning. It is a strategy that integrates reading, writing, and talk, and it ignites personal response to a text. The fictional character created by the author is made all the more real for students as they take on the perspective of that character.

It can be somewhat of a challenge to teach the students about voice in writing, but by becoming the "I" in the story by writing a fictitious journal entry, students are indeed using voice in their writing. Not only are students, through retelling, determining important events of a story, but they are making inferences about events and issues of the story, reflecting on issues and problems as a character in the story might experience them.

In-role journals give evidence that students are able to

- enter the world of the story
- dig deeply into plot, character, theme, and issues inherent in the novel
- imagine themselves as other people
- reveal empathetic understanding by stepping into the shoes of others
- demonstrate understanding of the thoughts, feelings, and problems of characters in a novel
- consider the vocabulary, language, and style used by the author
- write in the first person

I have used this activity in two different contexts:

1. students respond to the same novel
2. individual students respond to independent reading time

Tips for motivating in-role writing:
- The in-role activity can be done following independent reading time, as students retell in role something that happened in the novel they read.
- Students can write the journal entries about a single event in the novel or as a series of events over time.
- Entries may be written from the point of view of an animal or inanimate object.
- Students can write by hand or using the computer.
- Students might consider the format, the paper, the font, etc. of the original to bring authenticity to the journal entry.
- Creating illustrations or graphics for the entry is an option.

Because they are encouraged to express ideas in an open-ended way, because they are moving into the world of "as if," because they have the events of a story to motivate the writing, the students, upon reflection, have claimed this to be a favorite "book report."

Samples of Character Journal Entries

Dear Diary

Today the strangest thing happened. A little fox was taking me to the place Sylvie a) wrote her wish ricks b) hid our mother's flamingo mug. I know one of my father's 'Do Nots' is 'Do not touch ANY wild animal', but I TOUCHED THE FOX. How could I not?

> Jules (from the novel *Maybe a Fox* by Kathi Appelt and Alison McGhee)

Dear Diary

Oh no! Today is the day for play auditions! Do I really want to do this? I hope Ms. Udell will allow me to be Charlotte. Then maybe just maybe people will see that I'm really really a girl. I'm so glad by best friend Kelly wants me to be Charlotte too. I feel so much more comfortable now that she told me a lot of boys play a girl's part in plays. I have been waiting for this very moment for what feels like years ago. OK. Here goes nothing! I hope I get to play the part of the girl spider.

> George (from the novel *George* by Alex Gino)

Dear Diary

Today I feel rotten. Even though the sun is bright and the weather is warm, I feel absolutely terrible. My mouse family (called a mischief) tried to escape from 'that horrible place' but I was the only one who made it. I'm so small, how can I ever rescue them. Will I ever see them again? Being a mouse is so hard. I wish I was big like a human so I could have more rights. And now I have to find food for myself. Back in 'that horrible place' we never had to find our own food. They gave us everything but almost killed us in the process. OMG! Rats!! Looks like I'm about to become a meal.

> Isaiah (from the novel *Word of Mouse* by James Patterson and Chris Grabenstein

Drama Extension

I have found that an important follow-up to the assignment is to have the students share their responses with each other in role. In this way, the activity promotes talk response to the reading and writing experience, while it initiates drama exploration through improvised, in-role conversations. The following outline is a simple way to introduce in-role paired interviews:

1. Students work in pairs: partner A and partner B.
2. One person (partner A) silently reads his or her partner's (partner B's) writing.
3. Partner A then interviews the Partner B, who speaks in role as the novel character. Interviewer may be assigned a role: e.g., a relative, a media reporter, a neighbor, a babysitter, an employer of the character being interviewed.
4. The activity is repeated and reversed so that each person has a chance to be interviewed.

Additional Contexts for Perspective Writing

Beyond having students write a journal or diary entry from the point of view of a character, regardless of the story's time or setting, invite them to use their imaginations and write any of the following in character:

- A letter of advice to someone in the story; this letter could be written in the role of another character from the book.
- A letter to an advice columnist, describing a problem and articulating the feelings of the character; students, in pairs, could exchange letters and write back as the columnist offering suggestions on ways to handle a situation/problem.
- An e-mail from one character to another
- A message for a Facebook wall for a character in the story
- A newspaper, magazine, or media report about a real or fictitious incident derived from the story

RESPONSE JOURNALS

Larry's Class

No two persons ever read the same book.

— Edmond Wilson

A book doesn't make sense if nobody's reading it.
—Miranda, Grade 5, from *Text Talk: Towards an Interactive Classroom Model for Encouraging, Supporting and Promoting Literacy* by Larry Swartz (2000)

A reading response journal (also called a dialogue journal or a literature log) is a convenient and flexible tool whereby readers are helped to reflect on their reading and make comprehension visible. Having readers keep a journal invites them to communicate and explore the ideas and feelings that a text evokes and to relate what they read to their own lives. Journals provide a more personal forum for responding to literature as students reflect; the response tools also provide a medium through which individual students make choices on how to respond to the books they read.

Reading response journals place readers at the centre of their learning, serving as records of what the readers are thinking about texts. Journals provide space for learners to reflect on, interact with, and find personal meaning in works of literature. They encourage storytelling, questioning, imagining, and speculating. When used on an ongoing basis—consistency matters—they provide ongoing documentation about readers and their learning for both students as readers and for the teacher as audience and guide. A reading response journal is a powerful way to stimulate interaction among teacher, text, and learner.

Sharing journal entries with others can be entertaining and informative. A teacher, friend, or family member who reads selected entries can begin a dialogue with the novel reader by offering comments on the reader's responses, pointing out connections with their thinking and expressing their points of view. If students set up a journal entry as a letter, there is a particularly authentic context for someone to read and respond to it. It is not necessary that those who respond to journal entries have read the same text as the reader.

There are several ways in which a teacher can facilitate journal exchanges.

1. The teacher can establish a system where assigned reading buddies exchange entries.
2. The teacher can invite students to submit their journals for his or her reading. The activity can be structured so that the teacher is responding to five or six journals at any given time.
3. Students can be asked to place sticky notes on journal excerpts, inviting focused response to specific items.
4. Students can meet in groups of four or five to share entries of their choice, asking questions, making connections, or offering opinions of what has been offered.
5. The teacher may prompt students to share journal entries with a parent or other adult.

Any exchange of journals can lead to either written or oral book talk, thus extending the reading response journal entry. When a trusted audience responds to the journal, the reader can clarify thinking about the story, raise questions to explore further, and make connections between text and his or her life.

Students may choose to glue a list like this into their reading response journals for reference.

Suggested Journal Prompts

The following journal prompts can help students reflect on their independent leisure reading as they record responses to what they read:

1. What did you enjoy (or not enjoy) about what you read?
2. What, if anything, puzzled you as you read the text? What questions came to mind?
3. As you read, what did you "see" in your mind?
4. What problems unfolded in the novel? How do you think these problems will be resolved?
5. What words, phrases, sentences, or images made an impression on you. How so?
6. What interests (or does not interest you) about the characters in the novel?
7. How do the events and issues in the novel connect to your own experiences or those of someone you know?
8. What new information did you learn from reading the novel? What might you want to know more about?
9. How do you feel about the way the author presented the story?
10. What did you wonder about as you read the novel? Finished the novel?
11. What did you learn about yourself as a reader?
12. What might you tell others about what you read?

35-Word Novel Summary

title of book and author's name
2 words that express your opinion
3 names of characters
4 new words you learned by reading the novel
5 words that describe the setting
6 first words of the novel
7 words that summarize the main problem of the novel
8 words that summarize the plot of the novel

Pembroke Publishers ©2017 *Take Me to Your Readers* by Larry Swartz ISBN 978-1-55138-326-2

Poetry Is…:
Poetry as a Model for Student Writing

For me, poetry has always been a way of paying attention to the world.

— Naomi Shihab Nye

There is something about poems that is like loving children: They keep returning home and singing to you all your life.

— Felice Hollman

Poetry invites us to be.

— Sheree Fitch

For further ideas on writing poetry, see *The Poetry Experience* by Sheree Fitch and Larry Swartz, Experimenting with Form and Language (pp. 16–17) and The Poet Brain: 10 Activities (pp. 18–21).

Poetry Goes to School: From Mother Goose to Shel Silverstein by Bob Barton and David Booth is a comprehensive resource for teachers who are eager to fill their classrooms with poetry.

In the past decades, we have made great strides in the area of children's poetry, seeing the value of poetry both as a literary and an art experience. Using poetry can enhance learning not only for reading and writing, but also for discussing, questioning, performing, painting, singing, and dancing. There are many ways to make poetry an enjoyable classroom activity. Many teachers choose to give poetry a focus by implementing a poetry unit over two or three weeks where students are usually guided through writing poems according to formula patterns. This might be a place to start, but poetry, to be meaningful in the program, should be genre woven into a program all around the year. Poetry is not just a unit.

Over time (and over my thirteen or so years in a classroom environment), students should come to laugh, weep, question, pause, ponder, wonder, and experience poems for their potential to sharpen focus on the human and natural world, the heart, and the mind. Hopefully our classroom experiences help our students to collect a grab bag of poems that rest in their pockets and sing in their heads. These classroom experiences include not just writing poetry but reading all kinds of poems together and independently, responding to poems through talk and writing, using poems for both interpretation and improvisation in drama, creating art from poem words, introducing poems on a theme or a by a poet, discovering and uncovering a poem's meaning. As Archibald Macleish informs us, "a poem should not mean / But be."

Ten Ways to Experience Poetry

1. Choral Dramatization: large group

A poem is read as a whole class using a variety of choral techniques.

2. Choral Dramatization: small group

Group members divide the lines among themselves and work toward presenting the poem after many rehearsals.

---

3. Written Response

What does the poem make you wonder about? Feel?
What did the poem remind you of?
Why do you think the poet wrote this poem?

4. Talk Response

In groups, we can share our thoughts, questions, connections of the poem, the word choice, the form, etc.

5. Raising Questions

Ask questions arising from the poem to answer with others.
What questions might you ask the poet?
What parts puzzle you?

6. Pattern Writing

Use the form of the poem or rhyme scheme to write a poem.

7. Creating a Picture Book of a Poem

Create illustrations to accompany the text. Pictures can be assembled into a picture book or a PowerPoint or other presentation.

8. Choosing a Favorite Poem

Students read from anthologies independently and mark a favorite poem with a sticky note. Students can work in groups to share their favorites and give reasons for their choices. Poems can be transcribed onto chart paper and displayed around the room.

9. Poem of the Day

A poem-a-day can be an important ritual in the classroom, inviting exposure to a variety of forms, a range of poets, and a smorgasbord of words. A poem could be chosen from a single poet, a theme, or a poetic form. Students can select and present the poem to be read each day. At the end of the week, students can choose a favorite poem.

10. Defining Poetry

Students can write a personal definition of poetry in 25 words or less. Students are then paired up to compare definitions, then synthesize ideas to create a new definition of exactly 25 words.

HITCHHIKING ON POETIC FORMS

Larry visits Cynthia Duncan-Lumsden's Grade 4 Classroom

Providing poetic forms (e.g., haiku, cinquain, acrostic, limerick, concrete poems) provides a structure for teachers that encourages students to plunge into a pool of writing poetry. Poetry is not always a paint-by-numbers exercise in which we fill in spaces according to rules. When working as poets, we should be able to experiment with a varied palette, using the kind of word paint that we wish—and feeling free to go outside the lines. However, writing poems from a model can be a good way to *begin* writing poems, letting us play with patterns, manipulate words, count syllables, or comply with a specific meter or rhythm. Writing in this way becomes a puzzle for students to solve, as they model words and release their imaginations.

After sharing *Sometimes I Feel Like a Fox* by Danielle Daniel with students and having them listen to the twelve verses, it was quite easy to slide into a pattern-writing activity where the students filled in the blanks to create their own rhyming poem verses.

Samples from *Sometimes I Feel Like a Fox* by Danielle Daniel:

> Sometimes I feel like a bear,
> Strong and confident.
> I stand tall and growl
> And protect those around me.
>
> Sometimes I feel like a deer,
> Sensitive and kind.
> I listen for the sounds in the distance
> And prance through the forest.

Sometimes I Feel Like a Fox by Danielle Daniel is a picture book that was the 2016 winner of the Marilyn Baillie Picture Book Award. The book is an introduction to the Anishinaabe tradition of totem animals, and the speaker in the book explains why they identify with such creatures as fox, beaver, owl, or moose. The twelve verses in the book follow a distinct pattern.

Pattern-Writing Activity

1. Students name an animal of their choice.
2. Students brainstorm adjectives that might describe the animal.
3. Students list characteristics to describe appearance, characteristics, or behaviors.
4. Students write a sentence in first person voice to describe animal's appearance, characteristic, or behavior.
5. Students create their own rhyming verses by filling in the blanks in the pattern:

> Sometimes I feel like a _____,
> _____ and _____.
> I _____
> And_____.

Extensions

- Students present their poems chorally as monologues, perhaps adding sounds and movements.
- Students create an illustration to accompany poem. Poems are collected to create a class anthology or digital presentation entitled *Sometimes I Feel Like a Fox*.

Sometimes I feel like a snake
fast and patterned
I eat big mice
and slither away full!

Raven   by: Trang

Sometimes I feel like a Raven
Sneaky and mysterious
I can fly as high as an eagle,
and can keep the secrets that you tell.

By: Sonam

Monkey
Sometimes I feel like a monkey
playful and curious
I swing from tree to tree,
and have an addiction to bananas.

WRITING FREE VERSE POEMS

Larry visits Lisa Donohue's Grade 3 Classroom

I was invited to write a poem about bullying for an anthology entitled *Sticks and Stones* (Rubicon Publishers) and have had great success in sharing this poem with elementary students. The poem has helped them to consider how an animal can be like the bully or the bullied. By writing poems of their own, students gain understanding of metaphor and personification.

1. If you were going to write a poem about someone bullying, what animal might you choose to represent the bully or bullied (tiger, shark, snake, rabbit, deer, etc.)?
2. Jot down some characteristics that would describe this animal's appearance, behavior, personality, actions.
3. Consider how the animal is like a bully or bullied and write a sentence or two about this animal using some of the words from your list.
4. Transform this sentence into a free verse poem, by writing one, two or three words on a single line.

Mosquito

She's tiny.
She's mean.
She's cruel.
She fights.

The mosquito
Buzzes.
The mosquito
Bites.

She torments.
She swarms.
She teases.
She taunts.

The mosquito
Buzzes.
The Mosquito
Haunts.

You're bigger than her.
Your blood is what feeds.
Beware of the bully –
You're the victim she needs.

Cheetah

I am
the cheetah

I am
a
fast
fast
animal

I hunt
people
down.

It's hard
to excape
from
me!

Deer Hunt

A deer is
hunted by
us.

We eat them
and use
their
fright. We
take their
antlers.

They are
afraid.

Tiger

I am
The tiger
I am
big.

I have
sharp teeth
and
sharp claws.

I am
fast and
sneaky
like a
mouse.

You should
be afraid
of me

Poetry Is…: Poetry as a Model for Student Writing   91

I Screen, You Screen, We All Screen: Technology as a Medium for Response

The keyboard, the screen, the digital world are part of everyday reading and writing, constructing and viewing. Twenty-first–century schools have made vast progress in making technology available to students, whether access is in a technical lab, on moveable carts, with tablets for every student, or with students' own hand-held devices. "Technology in literacy education," David Booth points out in his book *Literacy 101*, "needs to be the 'new normal.'" Today's teachers recognize the need to offer their students opportunities to become computer-literate and use technology to support and enhance their own learning events.

📚 USING AN APP

Guest Voice: Randy Kirsh, Teacher-Librarian, Classroom Teacher, former Digital Literacy Teacher

When you see my students, I would hope your first thought may be, "These students are truly engaged in their work!" For me, however, it's not work you're observing, but an innate desire to learn. The key to creating these experiences is dynamic and authentic tasks in an encouraging and creative literacy program. This is what leads to enthusiastic students who are growing their literacy skills. It's the student's ownership of ideas, tasks, and their desire to learn. As a school and former board leader with technology, I often employ various technology tools and platforms to engage my students and redefine tasks to increase their 21st-century literacy skills. I hope that by sharing one such example, you might expand your pedagogy to include something similar for your students.

My reading program includes students creating reading responses to share their thinking and understanding of their reading. In any given month, students' reading responses focus on making connections, questioning, visualizing, inferring, determining importance, or synthesizing. Assessment for learning is gathered while we build our understanding of these ideas through class read-alouds, literature circles, and drama exploration. Instead of a day-by-day, week-by-week response, I invite students to prepare and share their reading responses with culminating monthly assignments. I employ a variety of technology to help engage students and instill a desire to learn—and share—with each other and the community.

Augmented reality is the real-time overlaying of digital content onto reality, viewed through a device such as a tablet, mobile phone, or headset. It enables the creation of extra content right at the spot. The following example of a reading response task using an app that thoroughly engaged the students helped to redefine my reading program. The students were invited to use augmented reality to share their thinking and understanding of what they had been reading for the month.

This month's task asked students to select a book in the mystery genre. In particular, the students were focusing on the concept of visualization. Leading up to the augmented reality culminating task, the students had had several opportunities to write responses and share their thoughts about visualizing what they had read. With the use of the augmented reality app called Aurasma (https://www.aurasma. com/) students published a short written response, reflecting on their reading from the month with an additional augmented reality layer.

When they shared their completed work, students' examples demonstrated what they saw beyond the words of the book. One student was reading a mystery and trying to find the killer. The original image without the augmentation showed the scene described in the book. With the augmented reality layer we were shown what the student visualized moments before the murder.

The class moved around with tablets and other mobile technology and were able to use the added augmented layer to share their thinking and visualizing. In another example, the augmented reality layer was an example of the student's connection to a local fire. When the technology was held over top, a burned-out fire was seen over the original image.

This is the true engagement and the love of learning that I look for in my assignments. It's authentic and 21st-century, and it encourages students to want to share their thinking with others in an real way. With the right tool, students will want to share their understanding of their reading and will engage in deeper, more meaningful conversations about their reading.

Tell Me:
Readers Retell Stories

Retelling helps students construct meaning from a text. In preparation for the retelling, they can revisit the text after an initial reading. This increased exposure to the text can clarify and confirm for students their initial perceptions. It also might lead students to discover that they need to modify or change these perceptions. Retelling can help readers re-evaluate the importance of one element or perhaps help them to see a connection between elements in the text. Once students are satisfied that they understand the text, that their perceptions are accurate, they retell what they have read to others.

Retelling is perhaps the ultimate strategy for teachers to use to monitor student comprehension of a story. Sitting one-on-one with individual students, teachers can invite students to retell a story that they have just read or listened to. Teachers can use a checklist to record whether students can

- name and identify characters in the story
- include details about the setting
- outline a sequence of events
- explain the problem in a story
- explain the solution to the problem
- identify a theme or lesson from the story

Oral retelling is perhaps the most authentic way to have students reveal their comprehension about a story (or movie, television show, theatre production, life event, etc.). A graphic organizer or a series of drawings can also be useful to guide students' retelling. Contexts for retelling the story collaboratively, in role, or with the use of props or artifacts are other ways to implement this strategy.

Five Strategies for Promoting Retelling

1. Cooperative Retelling

Students can retell a story that they have listened to, or read, together. To begin, students stay close to the plot of the original story. When the activity is repeated, students can add twists to embellish the story. One way to organize this is Round-Robin storytelling, in which each person in turn contributes to the narrative. Students are organized into groups and numbered off. On a prearranged signal, #1 from each group begins to retell until the signal sounds; then the #2 students take over; then #3; and so on. In this way the story is retold with no one person responsible.

Extensions
- An initial retelling may have students doing a basic, perhaps rushed, retelling. The activity can be repeated, inviting students to use as many specific details from the story they can think to include.
- Revisit the story to have students determine which details were omitted from their retelling.

- Students can retell the story and contribute details they think might embellish the story in describing the plot, character, and setting.

2. Retelling in Role

Option 1: Students consider who might be telling the story. Students can tell the story cooperatively using first-person narration, retelling the story from a particular point of view: *Tell the story through _____'s eyes.* Each group member assumes the role of a single character.

Option 2: Students work in pairs or groups of three to conduct an in-role interview with a character from the story. For example, the interviewer(s) can be representing the media interviewing a character who is retelling story events from a particular point of view. Events can be embellished to make the story seem as authentic as possible

3. Tableaux Stories

The technique of tableaux (still image) invites students, in groups, to physicalize a story by creating four to five sequential scenes to retell a story.

4. Storyboard

A storyboard is a kind of Story Map that serves a structured technique to help students sequence the events of a story.

Option 1: A graphic organizer is given on which students create a storyboard in panels. For primary readers, storyboards can include an image for each event that shows the beginning, middle, or end of the story. Older readers can create a storyboard using six to ten illustrations that retell the events of the story. A label or short narrative can accompany each illustration.

Option 2: Use two copies of a picture book for the storyboard, or scan and print pages. Illustrations are cut out and glued individually on cardboard. Students use the illustrations to create a sequence that retells the events of a story.

5. Story Boxes

Students gather or create objects or artifacts that can be used to retell a story. For example, for *The Very Hungry Caterpillar*, students can use pictures or small models of the different types of fruit that that the caterpillar encounters. Students are given a small box (e.g., shoebox) or a bag containing eight to ten items, each representing an episode or event in the story. Students prepare a retelling of the story by arranging the objects in order. Students should rehearse their storytelling before presenting it to an audience using the objects in the Story Box as props.

Bookshelf: Picture Books with A Sequential Pattern for Beginning Readers

Carle, Eric. *The Very Hungry Caterpillar* (Also *The Very Grouchy Ladybug*)
Cousins, Lucy. *I'm the Best*
Feiffer, Jules. *Bark, George*
Haughton, Chris. *Oh No, George!*
Henkes, Kevin. *Waiting*
Klassen, Jon. *I Want My Hat Back* (Also *This is Not My Hat; We Found a Hat*)
Klausmeier: Jesse; illus. Suzy Lee. *Open This Little Book*
Rosenthal, Amy Krouse; illus. Tom Lichtenheld. *Duck! Rabbit!*
Numeroff, Laura; illus. Felicia Bond. *If You Give a Moose a Muffin* (series)
Williams, Linda. *The Little Old Lady Who Was Not Afraid of Anything*

📚 STORY MAP

Larry visits Daniel Feldberg's Primary Special-Needs Classroom

Story Map apps provide templates for delivering a specific user experience to an audience: Esri Story Maps, built into ArcGis, are web applications that allows a reader to combine strongly visual maps with narrative text. A number of story map templates are available online. Any of these graphic organizers can provide some structure for students to retell a story. See https://storymaps.arcgis.com.

Shh! We Have a Plan by Chris Haughton is a perfect picture book for young readers. Repeated pattern ("ready one... ready two... ready three...") provides easy access to print; the challenge the four friends face in capturing a colorful bird in the woods adds suspense; the art (monochromatic blue with splashes of bright colors for the bird) adds to the narrative; limited text on a page make it ideal for reading together, reading with, and reading alone.

Story mapping is a strategy that most often uses a graphic organizer to help students retell or learn the elements of a book or story. Identifying story characters, plot, setting, problem, and solution, students read carefully to learn the details. An alternative to a graphic organizer is to have students create their own visual maps in an open-ended way. This allows students to reveal their understanding of story elements and organize it in their own way, sequential or not. Students might need reminding that the map they create will be used to have them orally retell a story to others.

I was invited into Daniel Feldberg's Primary Special-Needs classroom to read aloud two or three picture books and to provide a response activity that would have students respond to the story in a "creative manner." Of the books I shared, British author Chris Haughton's *Shh! We Have a Plan* seemed to engage the students the most. The simple text, the sense of adventure, the suspense and surprise all intrigued students and inspired them to ask me to read it again.

For a second reading, I encouraged students to act out the story in their own space in the classroom. The oral reading served as voice-over narration for them to become the characters in the story and dramatize the events. Since they performed without being watched, the activity invited them to successfully play out the story in their heads and through gesture and action.

A follow-up activity invited students to create a map, using markers and a large sheet of white paper, that would retell the events of the story in pictures and words. Since no graphic organizer was provided, the children could create a story map in their own way, representing characters and adventures that they thought would best tell someone about the story. Once completed, the children individually approached Daniel and/or me to retell the story. They were proud of their art work, with one boy giving himself an A+ that was displayed on his drawing (see sample on page 97).

A seven-year-old boy puts his creative energy into illustrating the moment of tension when the hunter attempts to capture the bird.

A Circle of Reading:
Group Responses through Literature Circles

Author Harvey Daniels offers support and a framework for implementing literature circles in the classroom. In *Literature Circles: Voice and Choice in the Student-Centred Classroom,* Daniels outlines the roles that help facilitate book talk. However, Daniel argues that assigned roles should be used sparingly if students are to talk authentically about books.

A literature circle is typically comprised of a small group of students who are reading a book and who meet to discuss, react, and share responses to it. When first establishing literature groups, the teacher may choose the same book for everyone to read. I recommend that you encourage students to choose among four or five titles that you make available to them. These titles may be by the same author or connected by theme. When it comes to assigning books for literature circles, some element of choice should be given so that students have a measure of control over their own learning: however, this isn't always possible, since some titles may be more popular than others.

To promote full participation in literature groups, some teachers begin by assigning roles that need to be explained and modeled. Then students switch role duties after each session until the formal roles are no longer required. Students can also benefit from demonstrations and exemplars of successful literature circles, where one group can serve as a model of how a literature circle can work or be improved upon. Suggested roles:

> **The Reteller** summarizes the reading for the group.
> **The Instigator** raises issues for the group to discuss
> **The Linguist** draws the group's attention to unfamiliar vocabulary and interesting words or sentences in the novel (including page number).
> **The Literary Artist** chooses an event or setting or mood conveyed in the reading and illustrates it for the group.
> **The Questioner** presents puzzling issues, questions, or wonderings relating to content, as well as personal response for the group to consider.
> **The Text Enricher** supports the text by bringing in related stories, nonfiction articles, or information from the Internet that can support or extend the novel's time, place, issues, and characters.

Success Criteria for Literature Circles

I can...
- ☐ Come prepared to a literature circle by making notes according to my assigned role.
- ☐ Successfully use my assigned role to present ideas about the book.
- ☐ Contribute ideas to discussions by making references to the book.
- ☐ Make connections to the book and to the responses of others, sharing personal stories and discussing other texts I am reminded of.
- ☐ Willingly offer my opinion about the book and in response to contributions of others.
- ☐ Give evidence from the book to support my opinions.
- ☐ Be attentive when others contribute to discussion.
- ☐ Help facilitate discussion by asking questions, negotiating ideas, solving problems, and telling stories.

DIGITAL LITERATURE CIRCLES

Guest Voice: Emanuele Barbaro, Grade 7/8 Teacher

Using Google Apps and Sites to implement Digital Literature Circles in my classroom provided me with the opportunity to create a structured, yet independent, environment centred on the students as they responded to books. In my previous years of teaching, I've found that literature circles provided an opportunity for students to engage in critical thinking as they read, responded to, and discussed books. However, it seemed over time that this became a somewhat tedious task for both me and my students. The number of templates available for implementing the various roles connected to literature circles required an abundance of photocopying, the students did not seem enthusiastic about the writing required to prepare for literature circle meetings, and often students did not seem prepared for these meetings. I strongly favor the intent of literature circles, and was ready to find a new way to implement the strategy in a structured but flexible way that promoted student autonomy for response.

My expertise in technology invited me to explore the alternative method of Digital Literature Circles. Intermediate students were familiar and comfortable with Google Apps, and I decided to venture into Google Sites to embark on the new initiative. My plan was simple in theory: Re-create my previous literature circle materials in an online format. This was done by developing a Google Site that was easily accessed by my students. Long gone was a printed-out page describing each literary circle role, now replaced with a link on the new Literacy Circle Website I created. The homepage of the website contained links to individual role instructions, resources, documents, templates, a sample webpage, and assessment material (i.e., rubrics). A class meeting was held to introduce the students to the website and I welcomed student suggestions about easier access to files, information, etc. As in the traditional literature circle procedure, I arranged students into groups of four or five, each assigned a novel. Consideration was given to strength of reading development, social skills development, and student interests to form the heterogeneous gender-balanced groups. An important procedure was to set up each group's individual website and demonstrate to students how to edit their webpage. I provided a demonstration of how to use Google Sites to edit and include text, photos, or information students thought relevant for discussion. To ensure that the procedure unfolded smoothly, students were given time to practice their site and to ask questions. They were quick to adapt to Google Sites Editor and, by the end of the first session, were efficiently editing their webpage banners, fonts, and templates.

The literacy circle unit was divided into seven week-long sections. Each week, an individual student took on an analysis role in the novel: the Questioner, the Word Finder, the Passage Picker, the Summarizer, and the Connector. Each role was associated with its own criteria and structure to extend students' understanding of the text and guide their discussion with peers. Each session was then further divided into specific literary devices that students needed to focus on each session: theme, symbols, setting, characters, climax, and author's message. Each session topic was explicitly taught so students had an idea of what an expectation for the week were. Literacy circles were set up on a four- or five-day plan:

Day One: Teaching the session topic, giving students an opportunity to read the assigned section of their novel.

Day Two: Short group discussion in which students have the opportunity to get feedback from their peers.

Days Three and Four: Completing assigned roles.

Day Five: Student discussion drawing from the contributions on the website.

This process is repeated until the completion of the novel.

I believe that the largest part of learning for students is how to develop a safe space for cooperative learning, where students can help each other out in making sense of a text. Literacy circles can teach students how to use the resources available for them and to become independent learners. The fact that students are allowed to select their own novel gives them the motivation to participate in the program; the sense of being a contributing member of the group keeps them motivated to complete their own individual tasks. The discussion period gives students a safe environment to share their learning and understanding of the text.

In the first session I heard a lot of the same voices speaking in each group but, as the weeks continued, more students were feeling comfortable with their group members and began to contribute their ideas as well. The organized sessions gave students a basis to focus their discussion and analysis. Finally, the use of the website as a collaborative tool made the literacy circles more engaging, as students were eager to add their thoughts and ideas to their own group's website.

Sample Student Entry

The Connector Role: Monique I

> I made a personal connection to an event in the novel to an experience that happened to me: the setting of the Barbadian town of shanties, and a fire that happened at my school in the 3rd grade. Again, this is not a physical connection, obviously, but instead an emotional one. In the book, the main character was set in a small town that was in a panic. There were people running and screaming everywhere because there had been an outbreak of zombies. One might think of this situation as a free-for-all, but the locals of the Barbadian town helped each other. They told everyone they saw to leave immediately, to save their lives, even if they didn't know them, or what they were going to do in the hazardous town. This situation somewhat relates to a fire that took place at my 3rd grade school. It was in Montreal on a bitterly cold day, and all the students were rushed outside into the freezing climate outdoors. There was no time to organize the classes, so there were students from the 3rd grade surrounded by those in 8th and 12th grade, in random patterns. All the students however, decided to make a giant huddle to brace from the cold, and none of us even knew each other. Age did not matter in the situation, we all just wanted the best for each other and we worked together to stay warm in the drastic temperatures. In both situations, relatively extreme events were happening, and they both showed the bond that even the most random of strangers can form, in a time of need.

I Just Want to Be Ordinary: Responding to Reading About Disability

If I found a magic lamp and could have one wish, I would wish that I had a normal face that no one ever noticed at all. I would wish that I could walk down the street without people seeing me and then doing that look-away thing. Here's what I think: the only reason I'm not ordinary is that no one else sees me that way.

— R.J. Palacio, *Wonder*

Voices into Action provides a spectrum of curriculum-based teaching resources and online tools to help teach older students (Grades 8 through 12) about prejudice, discrimination. and social justice, including a consideration of Human Rights and those who are disabled: http://www.voicesintoaction.ca

See *Dramathemes, 4th edition* by Larry Swartz, Chapter 8: Accepting Others (pp. 114–126) for a drama structure inspired by the novel *Wonder*.

What does it mean to be ordinary? What makes someone extraordinary?

As of this writing, the novel *Wonder* by R.J. Palacio has been on the *New York Times* Bestseller list for Middle Grade Hardcover Books for more than 100 weeks. In this novel, a boy named August (Auggie) Pullman, who has a facial deformity, is entering school for the first time. All he wants to do is fit in and be ordinary. By offering our students books about people who have a disability, we are giving them narratives that serve as case studies of those considered to be different. Such books have the potential to reflect on what being different means, what being normal means, and our attitudes to those who have physical or mental challenges. Novels such as *Wonder* can help build empathy and compassion in the hearts of young readers. And to create caring citizens of the world, it is important to serve our students literature that can guide them to confirm or challenge their assumptions about someone they know who is disabled, someone they read about who is disabled, or perhaps, like Auggie, someone who is living a life that is not "ordinary."

Bookshelf: Books about Extraordinary People

Picture Books

Bryant, Jen; illus. Boris Kulikov. *Six Dots: A Story of Young Louis Braille*
Carlson, Nancy. *Arnie and the New Kid*
Cottin, Menena and Rosana Faria. *The Black Book of Colors*
Fleming, Virginia; illus. Floyd Cooper. *Be Good to Eddie Lee*
Gilmore, Rachna; illus. Gordon Sauve. *A Screaming Kind of Day*
Keats, Ezra Jack. *Apt. 3*
Lears, Laurie; illus. Karen Ritz. *Ian's Walk: A Story about Autism*
Lyon, George Ella; illus. Lynne Avril. *The Pirate of Kindergarten*
MacLachlan, Patricia. *Through Grandpa's Eyes*
Munsch, Robert. *Zoom!*
Polacco, Patricia. *Thank You, Mr. Falker*
Shriver, Maria; illus. Sandra Speidel. *What's Wrong with Timmy?*
Thomas, Pat. *Don't Call Me Special*
Willis, Jeanne. *Susan Laughs!*
Yolen, Jane. *The Seeing Stick*

Other books by R.J. Palacio:
We're All Wonders
Auggie & Me: Three Wonder *Stories*
365 Days of Wonder: Mr. Browne's Book of Precepts

ANTICIPATION GUIDE

Larry visits Eric Williams' Grade 7/8 Classroom

The anticipation guide is a strategy designed both to activate a reader's background knowledge before reading a story or a nonfiction piece and to stimulate interest and build curiosity about a new topic. A list of statements about a topic is presented for students to consider and discuss with others. The statements are usually intended to arouse opinions, beliefs, and attitudes about a topic. Some of the statements might be considered true, based on students' experiences and assumptions. By circling Agree or Disagree about the statements, students can consider their own feelings and beliefs. To begin, students work independently to reflect on the statements. A follow-up discussion encourages students to share their opinions and, after listening to different opinions, some students may refine their understandings. After reading the text, students talk about the anticipation statements again, citing information from the text that supports or refutes each statement. Alternatively, students can respond once again to the statements provided in the anticipation guide and compare the answers they circled before reading.

The anticipation guide is a meaningful strategy to consider, articulate, and anticipate concepts connected to an issue, such as immigration, poverty, gender equity, bullying, families etc. Anticipation guides can be used as a minds-on activity, particularly for reading in the content areas. The activity provides a context to use predictions to promote learning from a text.

Teaching Tips

There are several ways to construct an anticipation guide. The following steps should be considered:

1. Identify major ideas and issues presented in the reading.
2. Consider beliefs and assumptions students are likely to have about the topic.
3. Write general statements that might confirm or challenge students' beliefs.
4. Instruct students to respond to the statements with either Agree or Disagree, a positive or negative response.

Anticipation guides can also be used as an activity before reading a novel, to help reveal some of the big ideas connected to the story theme. One Grade 5 class explored homelessness in preparation for reading *Mr. Stink* by David Walliams and completed an anticipation guide with statements about poverty. In a visit to a Grade 6 class, I used the anticipation guide on page 104 before reading the novel *Wonder* by R.J. Palacio. The statements in the anticipation guide probed significant points and led to a lively discussion in which students shared thoughtful responses about those who are considered to be disabled.

CONVERSATION ON PAPER

Larry visits Eric Williams' Grade 7/8 Classroom

Conversation on Paper is a strategy that invites students to have a conversation with someone, in silence, by exchanging thoughts on paper. The activity is best done in pairs so that students "dialogue" by responding to a partner's statements or questions. The activity can also be done in groups of three or four: students exchange papers with one another over a short period of time (i.e., 10 to 15 minutes).

The following is a sample response of a written conversation between two boys in a Grade 7/8 class. This strategy was introduced to engender a response to reading the excerpted text from the novel *Wonder*. In this passage, the description of August Pullman's physical features explicitly paints a picture of the boy who was born with Mandibulofacial Dystosis, more commonly known Treacher Collins Syndrome. The chapter begins with the following description:

> His eyes are about an inch below where they should be on his face, almost halfway down his cheeks. They slant downward at an extreme angle, almost like diagonal slits that someone cut into his face, and the left one is noticeably lower than the right.
> —R.J. Palacio, *Wonder*, "August Through the Peephole" (p. 88)

The response conversation is as follows:

Student 1: When I first read this, I felt bad for Auggie. Most people would probably stare at him. Then I thought he might be tired of all the pity he probably gets.
I don't know how I would treat him.

Student 2: I would treat him normally. I think that's what he would want.

Student 1: I think people do tend to stare at those who are different, but I'm sure those who are disfigured like Auggie may just get used to it.

Student 2: Maybe. Maybe not.

Student 1: I think I am one of those people who would do the 'look away thing' if I saw Auggie.

Student 2: Maybe. Maybe not.

Student 1: How do you think you would feel if you were this person?

Student 2: I know I would feel self-conscious.

Student 1: Yeah. I feel bad for Auggie, He couldn't even go to school because of his physical deformity.

Student 2: This makes me feel sad. I wonder what they will make this character look like in the movie.

Student 1: I want to read the book!!

Anticipation Guide

Read each statement and circle if you   AGREE (A) / DISAGREE (D) / ARE UNSURE (U)

1. I can tell someone has a disability by looking at them.	A	D	U
2. People in wheelchairs can play any sport.	A	D	U
3. A person who requires a wheelchair should not teach in elementary school.	A	D	U
4. It is best if people with disabilities were placed in special classes.	A	D	U
5. People who are deaf are unlikely to succeed in life.	A	D	U
6. People often stare at people who look different.	A	D	U
7. The word "disabled" is just a label that shouldn't be used to describe someone.	A	D	U
8. I feel comfortable when I meet someone I know has a disability.	A	D	U
9. Someone who needs to use a cane for walking has a disability.	A	D	U
10. Anyone can overcome a disability—even a mental health issue—if they work hard at it.	A	D	U

Finish the following statements:

11. When I hear the word "disabled" I think about…

12. When I see someone who is disabled, I wonder…

13. I am   ☐ ordinary or   ☐ extraordinary

Pembroke Publishers ©2017 *Take Me to Your Readers* by Larry Swartz ISBN 978-1-55138-326-2

Tech Time:
A Digital Approach to Global Issues

Inquiry is all about promoting enthusiasm for reading and writing, for learning, and for life. When we teach curricular topics and learning strategies through inquiry, students become both engaged and more competent as readers, composers and learners.
— Jeffrey D. Wilhelm, Peggy Jo Wilhelm, Erika Boas, *Inquiring Minds: Learn to Read and Write: 50 Problem-Based Literacy and Learning Strategies*

The need to discover can drive readers to find out more, to read a variety of genres, and to write in a variety of text forms in order to organize, revise, and present research to others. Curriculum topics, particularly in science, technology, and social studies, often provide a context for students to become engaged with a topic and embark on inquiry that connects students to an issue that is dependent on skills of reading, writing, and talk. Inquiry and investigation stimulate curiosity, arouse questions, and involve a research process for student to find answers or solutions to those questions. Inquiry can grow from a topic or theme, from students' interests, or indeed from a topic or issue they encountered in children's literature.

Bookshelf: Nonfiction Resources for Tuning in to Global Issues

DK Publishers/ Unicef: *A Life Like Mine: How Children Live Around The World*

Hearn, Emily and Marywinn Milne: *Our New Home: Immigrant Children Speak*

Hughes, Susan. *Off To Class: Incredible and Unusual Schools Around the World*

McCarney, Rosemary (with Jen Albaugh and Plan International). *Because I am a Girl: I can change the world* (Also *Every Day is Malala Day*)

Mulder, Michelle. *Yeny and the Children for Peace* (Also *Maggie and the Chocolate War*. See The Kids' Power Series, Second Story Press)

Smith, David J.; illus. Shelagh Armstrong. *If the World Were A Village* (Also *This Child, Every Child*. See the CitizenKids Series, Kids Can Press)

Strauss, Rochelle; illus. Rosemary Woods. *One Well: The Story of Water on Earth*

Walker, Niki. *Why Do We Fight?: Conflict, War and Peace*

Wilson, Janet. *Shannen and the Dream for a School* (Also *Severn and the Day She Silenced the World*)

Wilson, Janet. *Our Heroes* (Also *Our Rights*; *Our Earth*. See the Kids Making a Difference Series, Second Story Press)

Some Online Resources

Chris Daughtry. What About Now? (Song/Music Video) https://www.youtube.com/watch?v=roDXSHSEuoo

Prince Ea. Dear Future Generations: Sorry (Slam Poetry) https://youtube/eRLJscAlk1M

Newsela (Newspaper Articles) https://newsela.com/
Citizen Kid series, Kids Can Press http://www.kidscanpress.com/series/
  citizenkid

📚 VIDEO JOURNALS

Guest Voice: Marcie Lewis, Grade 6 Teacher

As an inquiry-based Grade 6 teacher, I frequently use collaborative tasks and discussion as instructional strategies to help facilitate student thinking and to build knowledge and skills. Many students enjoy these instructional strategies, but at times I have found that there are students who have wonderful ideas to contribute but don't respond to these instructional methods. To better meet the needs of all learners, I began using video journals as a tool for reflective thinking and assessment.

Video journals are short (under three-minute) recordings made using built-in webcams or digital recording tools to capture students' oral responses to a variety of question prompts. The prompts are designed to dig into students' thinking processes and understanding. Students are encouraged to formulate their responses to the prompts before recording, to assist in creating a high-quality product. Students may also choose to use basic video editing software (e.g., iMovie) to stitch together multiple clips, or may record one continuous clip. One affordance of video journals is that students can play back their own recordings and self-assess if the video is reflective of their best work, or if they need to record again. I have found that students generally improved their drafts more in the revising and editing stage of video journals than they did with traditional written journals, perhaps because of the multi-modal nature.

During a six-week transdisciplinary unit examining global issues, students were provided with thinking prompts to answer in the format of a video journal at various benchmarks in the unit. The first set of prompts was used for formative assessment and as a record of student thinking at the beginning of the process. Prompt selections included

- Why are you interested in your issue or why does your issue matter?
- What are you most looking forward to investigating within your issue?
- What do you think you might most need help or support with in completing your investigation?
- How could you imagine you might be able to take action and help make a difference related to your issue?

The next phase of the unit invited students to read nonfiction books available in the classroom library and the school library (see suggested list on page 105) to gather background information on the topic of choice. We also a watched YouTube videos that prompted a community discussion of global issues. Students were provided time over a three-week period to gather information from the library and the Internet to support their inquiry. At the conclusion of the research process, students responded to a second set of prompts. The focus of this set was having students self-assess how their thinking had changed based on their investigations and to document the knowledge that was developed.

Students selected global issues after exploring a variety of global issues as a class, examining current events in the media, studying the United Nations Sustainable Development Goals, and considering their personal strengths and passions. Examples of some of the global issues that the students explored:

- Deforestation: Deforestation can cause life-threatening situations for humans, animals, and the long-term health of the planet.
- Invasive Species: Prevention of the spread of invasive species is required to sustain healthy biodiversity.
- Technology and Society: It's crucial that we use technology responsibly, so we don't harm others, and to be aware of how technology is affecting our health, community, and, nature.

Students had access to various databases, library resources, and the Internet. Instruction was provided on examining sources for credibility and bias, as well as on using a variety of resources. As students became more knowledgeable about their issue, the use of specific terminology and evidence to support their ideas in their video journals increased. Students also enjoyed adding simple effects, such as titles and transitions, to help organize the various sections of their videos, or pictures to provide additional visuals to help explain their concept.

At this point, students applied their research and knowledge to create a piece of writing or media text that would best represent the big idea from their research. There was a wide variety of text styles chosen, from stop-motion animation to poetry to newspaper articles. To conclude the unit, students completed a final video journal to synthesize their thinking about the unit. They were encouraged to watch previous video journal entries and reflect on how their thinking had changed during the learning process.

This process was very informative for me as the teacher, as it allowed me to hear the voices of all students. As students had the time to formulate their ideas before recording their video journals, the answers to the questions showed deeper levels of thinking than I typically see in a classroom discussion. Several students who are not normally enthusiastic participants in class discussions produced excellent journal entries, expressing ideas that I would have not heard during discussion. For students who have stronger oral communication skills than written communication, the act of being able to talk and explain their thinking was beneficial.

Teaching is rooted in developing positive relationships with your students, and the use of video journals allowed me to better meet the needs of all learners in my classroom and establish positive relationships within my classroom community.

Am I in the Story?
When Readers See Themselves in Books

Not seeing one's self, or representations of one's culture, in literature can activate feelings of marginalization and cause students to question their place within society.
— Susan Landt, "Multicultural literature and young adolescents: A kaleidoscope of opportunity" in *Journal of Adolescent & Adult Literacy*

A Poem for Peter by Andrea Davis Pinkney, illustrated by Lou Fancer and Steve Johnson, is a tribute to Ezra Jack Keats and the creation of *The Snowy Day*.

To begin, a shout-out to Ezra Jack Keats, whose experience led him to create a picture book with a black child as a hero. For the 50th-anniversary edition of the book, Keats wrote

> None of the manuscripts I'd been illustrating featured any black kids—except for token blacks in the background. My book would have him there simply because he should have been there all along. Years before I had cut from a magazine a strip of photos of a little black boy. I often put them on my studio walls before I'd begun to illustrate children's books. I just loved looking at him. This was the child who would be the hero of my book.

The Snowy Day, awarded the 1963 Caldecott Medal, was named one of the most 100 Important books of the 20th Century by the New York Public Library. In his Caldecott speech Keats said, "I can honestly say that Peter came into being because we wanted him." Up until *The Snowy Day*, African-American children did not see others like themselves in children's books. More than 50 years later, the book industry has exploded with books that shine a light on a race, culture, and identity through fictional stories and illustrations that pay forward the work of Ezra Jack Keats.

While we could argue that any children's literature worth its salt broadens children's views of the world and introduces them to ways of looking at the world they might not otherwise have encountered, there are some books that do more than this. They give voice to individuals and groups whose perspectives are not often heard or respected. They show the effects of unequal power relations and celebrate those who make a difference in the lives of marginalized groups and individuals. They provide vicarious experience of diverse of ways of being and honor cultural diversity.

In recent years, publishers have given strong attention to books featuring populations that have felt victimized, oppressed, or discriminated against in some way. Across the community of children's book publishers, more and more books are being published that are recognized as *multicultural literature*, which tends to be considered as books that focus on race and ethnicity. However, an expanded definition of multicultural literature, according to my colleague Marie Jose Botelho, reminds us that attention must also be paid to gender, class, sexual orientation, ableism, age, religion, and geographical location.

In selecting multicultural literature for classrooms, it is important that we assess a particular book's potential for addressing social justice goals, combating intolerance, and fostering a sense of inclusion. When we make a conscious decision to share books of race, culture, and identity that provide a mirror for some of the students we teach, we are recognizing and respecting their cultures and promoting a strong personal connection for those students. And so, in a community of readers, fictional characters who represent or assert their cultural identity can help to open the minds of young readers to acceptance of differences.

When we read, our imaginations are creating pictures of what the print suggests. Visualization is an important strategy for helping readers make meaning of text. When we read a picture book, we get from the illustrator a single stab at matching or enhancing the verbal text. When reading a novel, however, the reader invents images that accompany the text. Visualization as a response strategy helps readers to "see" the characters, the setting, and the action. These visualizations come from personal experiences, from books and movies, and, indeed, from the imagination. Visualization is drawn from the *self* (Am I in the story?) and considers *other* (Do you see what I see?). When reading, no two visualized responses will ever be identical.

Bookshelf: A Sampling of Books that Represent Different Races/ Cultures

See Bookshelf lists in other units for multicultural booklists on such issues as gender, poverty, ableism, homophobia, etc.

The Association of Canadian Publishers has produced a detailed catalogue featuring more than 100 annotated titles of Canadian publications divided into selections for K–8 and for high school. The books are identified by one of seven diversity themes: Abilities; Aboriginal, First Nations, Metis and Inuit; Citizenship, Immigration and Place of Origin; Religion, Culture and Celebrations; Family; Gender Identity and Expression, LGBTQ; and Race, Colour, Ethnic Origin. See #WeHaveDiverseBooks Catalogue List available at www.publishers.ca/topgrade

Picture Books

Alexie, Sherman. *Thunder Boy Jr.*
Bunting, Eve; illus. Ted Lewin. *One Green Apple*
Campbell, Nicola; Illus. Kim La Fave. *Shi-Shi-Etko*
Choi, Yangsook. *The Name Jar*
De La Peña, Matt; illus. Christian Robinson. *Last Stop on Market Street*
Katz, Karen. *The Colors of Us*
Keats, Ezra Jack. *The Snowy Day*
Khan, Rukhsana; illus. Sophie Blackall. *Big Red Lollipop*

Lester, Julius. *Let's Talk About Race*
Polacco, Patricia. *Mr. Lincoln's Way* (Also *Mrs. Katz & Tush*)
Recorvits, Helen; illus. Gaby Swiatkowska. *My Name is Yoon*
Say, Allen. *Grandfather's Journey*
Suneby, Elizabeth; illus. Suana Verelst. *Razia's Ray of Hope*
Uegaki, Chieri. *Suki's Kimono.*
Watts, Jeri; illus. Hyewon Yum. *A Piece of Home*
Yee, Paul; illus. Jan Peng Wang. *A Song for Ba*

Middle School Novels

Alexander, Kwame. *The Crossover* (Also *Booked*)
Cavanaugh, Nancy. *Just Like Me*
Cervantes, Jennifer. *Tortilla Sun*
Curtis, Christopher Paul. *Bud, Not Buddy* (Also *Elijah of Buxton; Bucking the Sarge; The Mighty Miss Malone*)
Donwerth-Chikamatsu, Annie. *Somewhere Among*
Dumas, Firoozeh. *It Ain't So Awful, Falafel* (Also *Funny in Farsi*)

Ellis, Deborah. *The Breadwinner* (trilogy)
Flake, Sharon. *The Skin I'm In*
Grace, Lin. *The Year of the Dog*
Hussain, Asim. *Khadijah Goes to School* (Also *Sayf and Froggy*)
Kogawa, Joy. *Naomi's Road*
Lai, Thanhha. *Inside Out & Back Again*
Park, Linda Sue. *A Single Shard*
Reynolds, Jason. *As Brave as You*
Ryan, Pam Muñoz. *Esperanza Rising*

Sloan, Holly Goldberg. *Counting by 7s*
Weeks, Sarah and Gita Varadarajan. *Save Me a Seat*

Woodson, Jacqueline. *Feathers* (Also *Locomotion*)

Young Adult Novels

Alexie, Sherman. *The Absolutely True Diary of a Part-Time Indian*
Ellis, Deborah & Eric Walters. *Bifocal*
Myers, Walter Dean. *Monster*
Thomas, Angie. *The Hate U Give*

Yang, Gene Luen. *American Born Chinese*
Woodson, Jacqueline. *Brown Girl Dreaming* (autobiography)

In the picture book, *Big Red Lollipop*, the Pakistani author Rukhsana Khan tells a story, based on a true incident, of two sisters who attend a birthday party that is culturally different from the ones they are familiar with in their East Indian culture.

VISUALIZATION

Guest Voice: Marianna Di Iorio, Grade 2 Teacher

When we read, we imagine, and when we imagine, we visualize. When listening to a story or reading independently, we often create pictures in our mind suggested by the print. It is important to demonstrate visualization to our students, since it helps them understand that the mental images—the movies in our heads—that may emerge from our reading supports our meaning-making. When giving focus to this strategy, we also help students understand that we each build a visual world that is different from the one being built by the reader sitting next to us.

As a Grade 2 teacher, there are many parts of my day that I love. Without a doubt, though, the daily event I most look forward to is the time we gather together at the carpet for a story being read aloud. We all enjoy this time: the children are attentive and focused to listening as I, for one, enjoy the opportunity to read dramatically and to encourage discussion as we journey through a picture book. Picture books take us to places that are familiar and to places we can only imagine. They make us laugh, think, relax, and learn. It is often through these wonderful stories that we can take the time to think critically about the messages in texts.

Over the years, I have been particularly conscious of the need to share books in which children might see themselves. I have come to recognize an obligation to use books that represent different cultures. The picture books I choose to share each day are chosen with care. Sometimes the intention is to support curriculum, sometimes to draw attention to a genre or an author, sometimes to invite laughter or emotional connections. Ultimately, when I choose a picture book with representations that speak to my students, they show a special kind of close connection—an important one—to the book. For example, when I read *Big Red Lollipop* by Rukhsana Khan to my class, some students raised their hands with excitement to tell me who they know with the same name as the character in the story (Sana). One girl in the class eagerly announced, "That's me in the book!" As much as I recognize the importance picture books play in my literacy program, I also know that there are limitations to using them. Picture books are a product of a particular social context. As a teacher working in an inner-city school in Toronto with a diverse population of students, I recognize that the representations in picture books can never speak to every student in the diverse population I work with, despite our best efforts to acquire a diverse collection of books with a wide range of representations

Several years ago, when I was working as a teacher-librarian, I invited Bob Barton to my school as a guest storyteller. He had recently published *The Bear Says North – Tales from Northern Lands*. He began reading one of the stories from his book, not showing any of the illustrations. Then, partway through the telling, he stopped and asked, "What did you see inside your head as you listened to the story?" Bob asked students to describe the character in the story. Each person's response was different (of course!) Some saw her with blonde hair, others with long, dark hair. They were able to describe in detail their impressions of her clothes as well. Experienced readers do this out of habit. They create images in their heads from the words they hear. I saw how powerful this visualization technique was and have continued to use this strategy. By putting together their understanding of a character in their minds, based on their own experiences, students do something that picture books often can't: create more diverse characters. By allowing students to articulate their visualizations, we give voice to the diversity amongst our students.

I use variations of this visualization strategy throughout the year, in a variety of contexts.

As transitions are often challenging for young learners, at the beginning of the year I invite my students in and ask them to settle into their seats at their desks or at the carpet. I ask them to close their eyes and I take them somewhere with my words. Whether I take them for a walk in a forest, to a day at the beach, or on a walk through a busy city street, I try to engage all of their senses.

Next I invite them to tell me what they see, hear, taste, smell, and feel. They always have an answer, with each student having their own idea to add. Their articulation of the images in their minds shows me that they are listening, following along, and it encourages them to create more images in their heads, helping them along the path to become confident, experienced readers.

This is a mindful practice, a practice that takes us all on a journey together. I encourage students to expand their use of language, adding adjectives and adverbs to describe what they see in more detail. As the year progresses, my students know that I am looking to hear them use those "fancy" words when talking and writing. After a few short minutes with this exercise, my students are settled, calm, and ready to engage in their next learning task.

It's funny the things we can take from a Professional Development session, and I am grateful to Bob Barton for offering me the visualization strategy that I continue to use with stories and poetry. Giving my students opportunities to share their experiences, backgrounds, and visions through this technique gives me a chance to get to know them better, promotes their own personal expression, and creates a more caring, inclusive, and diverse environment where children can comfortably announce, "That's me in the book!"

All Together Now: Creating a Community Book

Hooray for Bill Martin Jr. and Eric Carle, whose book *Brown Bear, Brown Bear, What Do You See?* has been sandwiched between parent and child, teacher and young students, for millions of readers across the world since it was first published in 1967. The sequential question-and-answer pattern, the recognition of animals and colors, and the turn-the-page predictability have delighted and informed children about the potential of books for entertainment and developing reading skills. A perfect book!

The sequential patterns found in books are suitable springboards to student-written publications. When a pattern is repeated (see list below), it seems that the lesson plan for writing is in the book. The books become mentor texts for students to hitchhike their writing on. Pattern books build sight vocabulary and fluency. Having children write an innovation on the pattern is another way of reinforcing vocabulary and learning more about how verbal and visual text are formatted to bring meaning to the page.

Over the years, there have many teachers of young children who have had their students create their own versions of Bill Martin Jr.'s rhyming book. By changing the characters, asking a new question, and changing the characters again, children collaborate by contributing a page to the 'new' student-published book to read together.

Suggestions for Collaborative Books

1. **The alphabet** provides a convenient pattern for collaborative efforts. Each student can be assigned to create a page of an alphabet book. This can be as simple as identifying nouns or verbs for each letter of the alphabet. The names of animals, authors, book titles, or book characters are other examples of potential alphabet book creations. Many alphabet book patterns provide a suitable launch into writing: *Eating the Alphabet* by Lois Ehlert; *Tomorrow's Alphabet* by George Shannon and Donald Crews; *A My Name is Alice* by Jane E. Bayer and Steven Kellogg.
2. Each student contributes one page for **a class information book** on a topic studied in class (e.g., dinosaurs, recycling, safety).
3. Students can illustrate **a poem or song** by writing one line or stanza on each page and then providing an illustration for the verbal text. Possible texts include "Life Doesn't Frighten Me" by Maya Angelou (lines of poetry); *The Cremation of Sam McGee* by Robert Service (stanzas); *What a Wonderful World* (song verses).
4. **Collaborative Biographies** can be created, for which each student contributes a fact about a historical political figure or sports hero.
5. Students can create a picture book or chapter book story by having **each student retell one chapter** of the story.

Collaborative books can be transformed into a digital format, with each student's page featured as a slide in a PowerPoint or Google Slides presentation.

Bookshelf: Pattern Books

The authors of *Brown Bear, Brown Bear, What Do You See?* have been inspired to create new versions of the *Brown Bear, Brown Bear,* pattern:
Polar Bear, Polar Bear, What do you hear...
Panda Bear, Panda Bear, What do you see?...
Baby Bear, Baby Bear, What do you see?...

Burningham, John. *Would you rather...?*
Cousins, Lucy. *Hooray for Fish!* (Also *Hooray for Birds!*)
Daniel, Danielle. *Sometimes I Feel Like a Fox*
Daywalt, Drew; illus. Oliver Jeffers. *The Day the Crayons Quit* (sequel: *The Day the Crayons Came Home*)
Ewald, Wendy. *The Best Part of Me*
Harris, Annaka; illus. John Rowe. *I Wonder*
Martin, Jr., Bill; illus. Eric Carle. *Brown Bear, Brown Bear, What Do You See?* (series)
Parr, Todd. *Reading Makes You Feel Good* (Also *The Peace Book; The Thankful Book; The Feelings Book*)
Radunksy, Vladimir. *What Does Peace Feel Like?*
Thomas, Shelley Moore; photography, Eric Fultran. *Somewhere Today*

📚 COLLABORATIVE BOOK

Larry visits Ruby Bolognese's Grade 1 Classroom

A Collaborative Book is created when students work as a community (groups or whole class) to publish a book. Each student creates at least one page to contribute to the publication. Once a topic or pattern is decided upon, each student writes a sentence or a passage they think could be included in the book. When using a picture book as a source, it is important to draw attention to the syntactic pattern being used by the author. Students use the writing process to draft, revise, and edit their pages, before a final version of the text is ready for publication. Students then create illustration to accompany their text, using art media such as construction paper, torn paper, art, pastels, etc. Creating collaborative books is a useful bookmaking activity that builds community, puts the writing process in action, and offers a book to be read by class members (and others in the school community) as a shared-reading or independent-reading experience

Here are the different phases of the lesson that moved students from draft to published copy of a collaborative book, entitled *We Like to Read*.

1. Minds On: The question was posed, "Why do we need to read?" The teacher recorded student responses on a chart.
2. Sentence Stems: Students were each given a reproducible sheet with three sentence stems:

   Reading is important because...
   I like to read because...
   When I read I...

   Time was given for children to complete each statement.

This activity could have been simplified by having a single sentence stem to complete (e.g., *We need to read because...* or *Reading is important because....* Giving students a choice of statements to work on allowed more variety in syntactic pattern for the final publication.

3. Revising and Editing: Students each chose one statement from their draft writing. Children conferenced with teacher and myself to move to a second draft. At this stage, they needed support in transcribing ideas. Also, conferencing encouraged many students to elaborate on their initial response. For example, *Reading is interesting* is a suitable simple sentence, but when asked a probing question, students expanded to the sentence by adding a thought: *Reading is interesting because you can get new ideas for your own stories.*

4. Teacher Read Aloud: The book *Reading Makes You Feel Good* by Todd Parr was shared with the students. Attention was drawn to text features that included single statements spread across the top of a page and simple vibrant illustrations that accompanied the verbal text.

5. Publishing a Page: Each student was given a bright large sheet of paper to create one page to contribute to our collaborative book. Most children were ready to move their draft copy to published copy of a page with verbal text and illustration, using black markers. Some children needed further guidance to present ideas clearly with standard spelling and grammar.

6. A Collaborative Book: The book was assembled into a final published format, with each child having made a contribution. Each student had the opportunity to read his or her statements aloud.

   The creation of the book represented a true collaborative effort and demonstrated authentic responses to reading:

> *Reading is important because you can imagine you're anything like Gregory from Diary of a Wimpy Kid.*
>
> *Reading can be fun because you can imagine you are a king in a castle.*
>
> *We need to read because we can learn about make-believe and not-make-believe stories.*
>
> *When you read you grow and get big.*
>
> *Reading is important because it makes your brain think.*
>
> *Reading is fun because you can learn about Space and the Earth and Stars and the Planets and the World.*

4

Connected by Theme

A thematic approach to learning combines structured, sequential, and well-organized strategies, activities, children's literature, and responses to expand a particular concept. A thematic unit can be considered multidisciplinary and multidimensional, tapping into the interests, abilities, and needs of students and respectful of their developing aptitudes and attitudes. In essence, a thematic approach to learning offers students a realistic arena in which to pursue learning, using a number of contexts and experiencing a range of print materials. The topic for a thematic unit should be broad enough to allow for a range of research and response, but not so broad that students will have difficulty linking concepts that are related to the unit. When selecting a theme, consider

- the curriculum
- students' interests
- relevant issues and big ideas
- print resources available (in a variety of genres)
- opportunities to integrate reading, writing, talk, media, etc.

For Your Consideration

☐ What is the value of teaching with themes?
☐ What are some challenges of teaching by theme?
☐ How do you gather resources to support the theme?
☐ How does literature play a part in thematic teaching? Which comes first: the book or the theme?
☐ What opportunities are there for integrating response activities through themes?
☐ What opportunities are there for connecting to other subject areas (math, social studies, science, health, etc.)?
☐ How do you go about planning a thematic unit?
☐ What opportunities are made available for students to work independently? With a partner? In small groups?
☐ How might you celebrate and/or share the theme with others?

What's in a Name?
Books Help Readers to Consider their Identities

There is nobody on earth with the same name as me. I am the only Thunder Boy who has ever lived.

— Sherman Alexie, *Thunder Boy Jr.*

Our names are artifacts of who we are, where we come from, our ancestry and our family stories. The connection between identity and how we represent ourselves can begin to be explored through our names, which serve as markers of our identity.

—Belarie Zatzman (professor at York University) in *Dramathemes*
4th edition by Larry Swartz

As literacy teachers, we strive to help students build bridges between the ideas in a text and their own lives. By asking the questions, *What stories do you have about the word _____? How does this book remind you of experiences in your own lives, or the life of someone you know?* we are helping students to access information, stories, and sometimes emotional responses to a text (or visual images). When these stories are awakened in the head before, during, or after reading a picture book, for example, and are invited to be revealed with others, we are activating text-to-self connections. Such connections help students make meaning with the text and we are offering them a significant reading strategy that they will use for life.

Everyone has a name. Behind every name is a story. Having students reflect on their names is a useful classroom event for encouraging students to consider their own identities. When we invite students to share their stories about their names, we are building community and enriching connections amongst group members.

Bookshelf: Books on Identity

Alexie, Sherman; illus. Yuyi Morales. *Thunder Boy Jr.*
Bayer, Jane E.; illus. Steven Kellogg. *A My Name is Alice*
Bruchac, Joseph; illus. Rocco Baviera. *A Boy Called Slow*
Choi, Yangsook. *The Name Jar*
Henkes, Kevin. *Chrysanthemum*
Mobin-Uddin, Asma; illus. Barbara Kiwak. *My Name is Bilal*
Mosel, Arlene; illus. Blair Lent. *Tikki Tikki Tembo*
Recorvits, Helen; illus Gabi Swiatkowska. *My Name is Yoon*
Seeger, Laura Vaccaro. *Walter Was Worried*
Williams, Karen Lynn, and Khadra Mohammed; illus. Catherine Stock. *My Name is Sangoel*

NAME STORIES

Larry visits Ahren Sternberg's Grade 5/6 Classroom

1. Teacher Tells a Story

To begin, I told the students a story of my name:

> At the time of my birth, for business reasons my father legally changed our family name to Swartz from Gwartz. So often, when people say my name, it is pronounced "Shwartz" but there is no 'h' in my name. The name Lawrence appears on my birth certificate, but I have always been known as Larry, and no documents, other than my driver's license, seem to have the name Larry. I was named after a cousin of my mother's.

2. Thinking about Our Names

I then asked the students to think about their own names and consider the significance of the name, the spelling of the name, how they got their name, etc. The What's in a Name? questionnaire (see page 119) helped students to reflect on different aspects of their name stories. In some cases, students might not be able to answer a question on the spot, so they were welcome to leave parts blank. By the question having been raised, students could contemplate an answer and perhaps find a question for further inquiry.

3. Sharing Stories in Pairs

As a follow-up to completing the sheet, students worked with a partner to share their answers to the questions.

4. A Community of Stories

Following the paired conversation, students volunteered to share their stories. However, if time allows, a successful community building activity would be to have students sit in a circle to share a name story. Some things to consider when stories are shared:

> What are some commonalities in the stories?
> What are some surprises encountered in the shared stories?
> What do stories tell us about equity and diversity?

5. Writing Our Stories

The lesson concluded with each student having the opportunity to write a name story, using any information they shared with others.

6. Interactive Read-Aloud

The picture book *Thunder Boy Jr* by Sherman Alexie was read to students. In this story, a young Indigenous boy, hoping not to inherent his father's name, wants to choose a name that celebrates his talents; e.g., "Full of Wonder." The book inspired a discussion about respecting the names we have been given, passing names on from generation to generation, celebrating identities, and family relationships.

Extensions

- Interviewing a Parent: Students use the What's in a Name? questionnaire to conduct an interview with a parent (or family member) about his or her name.
- Inquiry: Students find out more about their names by a) interviewing a parent, or b) using the Internet to find the meaning or derivation of the name.

The following are some samples of name stories the students wrote after sharing them orally:

My Mom is pregnant. The family is having dinner and they are talking about my name. My parents wanted to name me Emily. My Grandpa spoke up and said, "Emily isn't a strong enough name. Her name should be Katie if it's a girl!"

My middle name is Hoi. Hoi is a Cantonese name that means "open" and "little boy pig." My sister's middle name is Phoon, which means "little girl pig." And my cousin's middle name means "fat pig," I always feel sorry for my cousin. My nickname is Hoiboy. I got that name from my sister who wanted to annoy me. This story may be true or something my grandparents made up.

My name is Mia and I love it! My parents were going to name me Summer because I was born on summer solstice. I'm glad they named me Mia.

My name is Lhasa. It means place of the gods.

My Mom and Dad named me Jeremy because they each had to make a list with three names on it. They both had the name Jeremy on the list.

Once upon a time there was a kid blessed by God, and thus born as Adam.

My name is Chinzee. My older sister calls me Chin. When I was a little kid many children bullied me and always called me Chinny. If I could have chosen my own name it would be Katrice because it is unique.

My name is Georgia. In Latin it means "farmer's daughter." My parents chose that name because my dad LOVES music (me too!). When my mom was thinking of girl names, she thought of Georgia and of course my dad loved it because of the Jazzy song "Georgia on My Mind."

When I was born, my parents named me William Emerson Phan. I am named William because of my Grandpa who died. I am named after the Emerson radio company (My dad loved radios). Phan is a Vietnamese name from my mom's side of the family. My last name is European. I have four names because in Asia it's lucky to have four names.

Here is a story about four characters named 'N' 'A' 'D' 'I'. One day N was taking a walk through the park and she bumped into A. So N and A walked together and then they met D. So they three of them walked and talked through the park until they were joined by I. They four friends came upon a lonely A, so they decided to go up her and chat to her and cheer her up. Soon after, they all became NADIA. Which is my name!

What's in a Name?

The following questions will help you think about the significance of your name. You can leave any items blank if you can't think of an answer.

1. What is your full name?

2. Do you know your name in any other language(s)? List.

3. What is the story of how you got your name? Were you named after someone?

4. What is the meaning of your name?

5. Do you have a nickname? What is it? How did you get this nickname?

6. Do you like your name? Why or why not?

7. If you could change your first name, what name might you choose?

8. What is the name of a pet you know? How did the pet get its name?

9. Do you know any family members, celebrities, historical figures, authors, or fictional characters who share the same first name as you?

10. What, if anything, is unique about the spelling of your first name? Your last name?

Pembroke Publishers ©2017 *Take Me to Your Readers* by Larry Swartz ISBN 978-1-55138-326-2

The Refugee Experience:
Exploring a Global Issue through Literature

Brave is waiting and believing in your heart that everything will be okay.

—Angela May George, *Out*

What will my future be?

— Marsha Forchuk Skrypuch with Tuan Ho, *Adrift at Sea:*
A Vietnamese Boy's Story of Survival

Once there was a boy who had to leave his home... and find another.
In his bag he carried a book, a bottle, and a blanket.
In his teacup he held some earth from where he used to play.

—Rebecca Young, *Teacup*

When offering students the opportunity to read literature about refugees, we are helping them not only to look outside their windows, but also to open doors to empathetic understanding and compassion for those who have been forced to flee. The theme explores the thoughts and feelings of people who have lost their homes and can never return to them again.

How can we ever reconcile losing our homes? How can those who are forced to leave their countries move forward step-by-step to find shelter and belonging, to strengthen their identity and culture, and to maintain pride and independence? By considering the plight of fictional and real people, this theme helps students wrestle with how we, as a society, can take responsibility for those citizens of the world who are refugees. Through fiction and nonfiction, students can come to develop and deepen their understanding of the refugee experience, and come to appreciate the place called home and the spirit called hope.

Bookshelf: The Refugee Experience

Picture Books

Argueta, Jorge; illus. Alfonso Ruano. *We Are Like the Clouds (Somos como las nubes)* (poetry)

Cha, Dia; illus. Chue and Nhia Cha. *Dia's Story Cloth: The Hmong People's Journey to Freedom*

Danticat, Edwidge; illus. Leslie Staub. *Mama's Nightingale: A Story of Immigration and Separation*

Del Rizzo, Suzanne. *My Beautiful Birds*

George, Angela May; illus. Owen Swan. *Out*

Hoffman, Mary; illus. Karin Littlewood. *The Colour of Home*

Kuntz, Doug and Amy Shrodes; illus. Sue Cornelison. *Lost and Found Cat: The True Story of Kunkush's Incredible Journey*

Lofthouse, Liz; illus. Robert Ingpen. *Ziba Came on a Boat*

Park, Frances and Ginger; illus. Debra Reid Jenkins. *My Freedom Trip*

Robinson, Anthony, Annemarie Young; illus. June Allan. *Mohammed's Journey: A Refugee Diary* (Also *Hamzat's Journey, Gervelie's Journey*)

Ruurs, Margriet and Falah Raheem (translator); illus. Nizar Ali Badr. *Stepping Stones: A Refugee Family's Journey*

Skyrypuch, Marsha Forchuk, with Tuan Ho; illus. Brian Deines. *Adrift at Sea: A Vietnamese Boy's Story of Survival*

Sanna, Francesca. *The Journey*

Trottier, Maxine; illus. Isabelle Arsenault. *Migrant*

Watts, Jeri; illus. Hyewon Yum. *A Piece of Home*

Williams, Mary; illus. R. Gregory Christie. *Brothers in Hope: The Story of the Lost Boys of Sudan*

Williams, Karen Lynn and Khadra Mohammed; illus. Doug Chayka. *Four Feet, Two Sandals.*

Young, Rebecca; illus. Matt Ottley. *Teacup*

Novels

Applegate, Katherine. *Home of the Brave*

Bondoux, Anne-Laure. *A Time of Miracles*

Burg, Ann E. *All the Broken Pieces*

Flores-Galbis, Enrique. *90 Miles to Havana*

Gratz, Alan. *Refugee*

Lai, Thanhha. *Inside Out and Back Again*

Mead, Alice. *Girl of Kosovo*

Paterson, Katherine. *The Day of the Pelican*

Pinkney, Andrea Davis; illus. Shane W. Evans. *The Red Pencil*

Stine, Catherine. *Refugees*

St. John, Warren. *Outcasts United: The Story of a Refugee Soccer Team that Changed a Town*

Nonfiction

Clacherty, Glynis. *The Suitcase Stories: Refugee Children Reclaim Their Identities*

Ellis, Deborah. *Children of War: Voices of Iraqi Refugees*

Goode, Katherine. *Jumping to Heaven: Stories about Refugee Children*

Hearn, Emily and Marywinn Milne (eds.) *Our New Home: Immigrant Children Speak*

Leatherdale, Mary Beth; illus. Eleanor Shakespeare. *Stormy Seas: Stories of Young Boat Refugees*

Naidoo, Beverley (ed.). *Making It Home: Real-life Stories from Children Who Flee*

FOUR-RECTANGLE RESPONSE

Guest Voice: Rachael Stein, Grade 6 Teacher

I experienced the following strategy while attending a reading conference and it has since become a favorite in my program, since it helps students to pause and reflect on their reading and reveal responses in writing that they can share with others in writing, then in conversation. For me, this strategy serves as an ideal integration of reading, writing, and talk.

In this activity, students use a graphic organizer to write a response after reading or listening to a story, a poem, an article, or media. By sharing their response in small groups, students can discover whether others' opinions and/or connections were similar to or different from their own. This activity works best if students work in groups of three.

1. Students take a blank piece of paper and fold it twice, to make four rectangles. They number the spaces 1, 2, 3, and 4.
2. In space 1, students write a short response to the text to consider what it reminded them of, to share their opinions, or to raise questions or puzzles.
3. Students exchange their organizers with another person in the group. Students read the response in space 1 and then write a response to it in space 2. What did the response in space 1 encourage them to think about? Students can agree or disagree with what was written.
4. The activity is repeated. Students read both responses on the sheet they receive and write a response to it in space 3.
5. The sheet is returned to the person who wrote the first response. Students read all three responses on the sheet and write a new response in space 4.

I'm reminded of the book 1 "The Breadwinner" and "I am Malala" because both have a story about living in fear and overcoming it with courage and Hope.

I feel that war should be gone 2 and only Happiness should be in the world.

I agree that war 3 should end because we should alwase be happy evrywhere and not scared.

"I wonder how hope and 4 courage can come a long even from the smallest speck can change the world forever".

6. In groups, students discuss the text, using their written responses to frame the discussion.

Tips

- Sentence-stem prompts could be offered to students to record their responses.
- Encourage students to write their responses as if they were having a conversation, connecting to what has been shared.
- Allowing three to four minutes for each written response encourages students to fill in the space with more than one thought.

In *Out* by Angela May George, illustrated by Owen Swan, people stare at a young girl, who is called an asylum seeker, but not her real name. The girl has seen horrible things and along with her mother journeys on a boat and finds refuge in a place where she enjoys winning races, the smell of the ocean, and a safe place to live. The girl longs to be reunited with her father, who did not make the trip with his family.

- Following the discussion, students can write a final written reflection, synthesizing the ideas that they've read or heard about.

The story of immigration and refugees is universal, and events in the media provided the class with authentic and particular accounts of Syrians who were forced to flee and seek asylum in other countries. Newspaper articles were shared that helped students make sense of the complicated (and political) issue of those desperate for help, and those who choose to reach out to help.

The stories in several picture books provide case-study accounts that help students work toward an understanding of refugees. The book *Out* was read aloud to students and they were guided through the activity described above. The following excerpts of student responses demonstrate their connections, their puzzlements, and their emotional responses to the story:

> I feel heartouched cause when she meets her dad the whole story gets more happy.

> I feel thankful that I live in a safe place and that I didn't have to go through something like that. I like the dark and mysterious textures and colours that were used in the book. It reminds me of my cottage.

> I wonder what happened before the boat and if it was a war, which war were they in?

> I wonder why was the dad in a different place than his family.

> I feel like if we stayed strong and thought of good things, we would have HOPE. Hope would get us through the hard times.

> I feel very touched and sort of confused because the ending was not really showing the way she feels about her dad coming.

> I'm reminded of the movie Batman Begins when Bruce Wayne was stuck in a hole where no one escapes but he stayed strong and waited, trained, tried, failed, tried again and finally got out.

Cry, Heart, but Never Break:
Making Personal Connections to Books

I loved my friend
He went away from me
There's nothing more to say
The poem ends
Soft as it began –
I loved my friend.

— Langston Hughes

The curtains were blowing in the gentle morning breeze.
Looking at the children, Death said quietly, "Cry Heart, but never
break. Let your tears of grief and sadness help begin new life."
Then he was gone.

— Glenn Ringtved, *Cry, Heart, But Never Break*

The Best Response to a Story is... to tell another story.

— Margaret Meek

The stories of our lives are swimming in our heads. When we talk with others, these stories pop out of our mouths, released by the human need to share them with others. When we are at social gatherings, at family celebrations, at dinner, on the street, in the hallways of the school, or in an office, staff room, or mall, we tell stories about what has happened to us, to people we know, or to people we've heard or read about. Sometimes a book, movie, play, or news report reminds us of things that have happened to us. Often, when others tell their stories, ours are awakened, and when we are comfortable with people we choose to reveal the stories that swim in our heads.

In the classroom, there is usually no specific instruction for these in-the-head narratives escaping and being revealed to others. Teachers and their students have a treasure chest of stories waiting to be unlocked and shared. When students tell personal stories, they are not only choosing to tell their about their life experiences, but they are also building a dimension of who they are.

Narrative, according to Harold Rosen, is an important mode of thought that helps us to order our experiences and construct reality. It is the teacher's responsibility, therefore, to give time and attention for students to use narrative in their thinking, speaking. and writing in order to develop the full range of their cognitive and emotional abilities. Unless young people are given opportunities to tell their stories, they may never come to understand or give meaning to them. Oral narrative is a powerful way of validating one's life to others. What may first be fleeting experiences gain significance when told aloud.

The stuff that we read is often the most significant way to inspire oral narrative in the classroom. This can particularly happen when students gather together to

"Each time a child describes an experience he or someone else has had, he constructs part of his past, adding to his sense of who he is and conveying that sense to others."
— Susan Engel, *The Stories Children Tell*

listen to a picture book being read out loud. Inspired by the picture book *Each Kindness* by Jacqueline Woodson, students can share stories about a time they were kind to someone or someone was kind to them. *I Know Here* by Laurel Croza can inspire storytelling about times we have moved in our life. Matthew Van Fleet's *Dog* can initiate students' stories about their pets. Good books can help students raise questions about sensitive issues or possibly find answers to some of their questions. A good book can support adults who are concerned, but perhaps uncomfortable, about discussing important issues such as dying and death. No one book can provide all the answers to a topic like death, but a good book can let students know that it's okay to talk about our feelings, our curiosities. A book about loss can encourage students to say what they are thinking and feeling days, weeks, and perhaps months following the loss. In a classroom setting, there may be comfort in the shared responses and shared stories about death and sadness.

The classroom needs to become what David Booth calls a "story tribe" in which students validate one another's experiences as well as explore shared meanings. We use a range of comprehension strategies to make meaning but, for me, text-to-self connections predominate. When students can connect with a text and say out loud—or perhaps keep inside the head—"That reminds me…," then the book has significantly done its job of making meaning and engaging the reader.

Inspiring Oral Narratives

1. Literature read-aloud to the class
2. Before the story: activating prior experience
3. During the story
   - encourage spontaneous responses: we cannot plan for what will trigger a memory
   - teacher think-aloud demonstrates how a story has inspired a text-to-self connection
4. After the story: Was there anything in the story that reminded you of something from your own life, or someone you know?
   - a word: e.g., *prize, award, trip, seashore, lost, moving, stitches*
   - a topic or question: e.g., *Have you ever been in danger? What happened? / Have you ever been afraid? Why? / Share a story about your name.*
   - an artifact: e.g., a photograph, an article of clothing, a toy, a book
   - story shared by someone else

Teaching Tips

- Students can share stories in small groups before sharing them with the whole class (or vice versa).
- When students tell stories orally, they are rehearsing a way to share their thoughts in writing. In many cases, it is important for students to write a personal narrative (memoir) to help give significance to the story. In this way, the event is a meaningful way to integrate reading (the book), speaking (oral narrative), and writing (memoir).

Bookshelf: Books about Death and Loss

Picture Books

Brown, Margaret Wise; illus. Christian Robinson. *The Dead Bird*
Jeffers, Oliver. *The Heart and the Bottle*
Lunde, Stein Erik; illus. Oyvind Torseter. *My Father's Arms Are a Boat*
Ringtved, Glenn; illus. Charlotte Pardi. *Cry, Heart, But Never Break*
Oskarsson, Bárður. *The Flat Rabbit*
Rosen, Michael; illus. Quentin Blake. *Michael Rosen's Sad Book*
Thornill, Jan. *I Found a Dead Bird: The Kids' Guide to the Cycle of Life and Death*
Varley, Susan. *Badger's Parting Gifts*
Viorst, Judith; illus. Erik Blegvad. *The Tenth Good Thing About Barney*

Novels

Appelt, Kathi and Alison McGhee. *Maybe a Fox*
Benjamin, Ali. *The Thing About Jellyfish*
MacLachlan, Patricia. *Edward's Eyes*
Paterson, Katherine. *Bridge to Terabithia*
Ness, Patrick; illus. Jim Kay. *A Monster Calls*
Pennypacker, Sara; illus. Jon Klassen. *Pax*
Rylant, Cynthia. *Missing May*
Smith, Doris Buchanan. *A Taste of Blackberries*

Young Adult

Asher, Jay. *Thirteen Reasons Why*
Green, John. *The Fault in Our Stars*
Jocelyn, Marthe. *Would You*
Nelson, Jandy. *I'll Give You the Sun*
Niven, Jennifer. *All the Bright Places*
Zusak, Markus. *The Book Thief*

📖 ORAL NARRATIVE

Larry visits Trina Tran's Grade 4/5 Classroom

Cry, Heart, But Never Break by Glenn Ringtved, illustrated by Charlotte Pardi, is a story about four young children who must cope with the loss of their grandmother, who on her death tells her grandchildren that it's all right to feel sad, but life will go on. Death appears as the Grim Reaper and tells his own story about learning about joy and delight, sorrow, and grief.

My visit to a Grade 4/5 classroom provided an opportunity for students to share personal stories about death. Before reading the picture book *Cry, Heart, But Never Break*, I shared my own stories, telling the students about my nephew Solomon who died of cancer at 33 years of age, and about the death of a special colleague, Brian, whom I often think about when sharing a good book. The stories that I told seemed to inspire some students to share their own stories about pets, relatives, or acquaintances who had passed. We heard about Brad's goldfish that was flushed down the toilet, Adam's dog who had recently been euthanized, Emma's Uncle Mohammed from India who died from kidney cancer, and Adam's grandfather who needed a tank to help him breath in the final years of his life. Students' shared stories triggered other narratives. For example, when Sonja told a story about her 98-year-old grandmother who was left alone for two days before anyone knew she had died, Zachary told a story about his 99-year-old Aunt Rose who was just about to celebrate her 100th birthday. Aunt Rose did not want a party to celebrate. Her family insisted. Aunt Rose fought back, saying she did not want a party, and one week before the planned party, she died. Stories begat stories. The class was becoming a story tribe.

The picture book was read aloud to the students without interruption. I instructed the students to be aware of what was happening in their heads as they listened to the story. The students were very familiar with text-to-self connections and terminology, and I told them that stories would likely pop up unexpectedly as they listened to Ringtved's narrative. Following the reading, we discussed the personification of Death. The community of readers revealed their stories, first as a turn-and-talk to discover what those around them were thinking and subsequently as a class discussion.

As a final activity, students were instructed to write a story, inspired by the picture book and the personal out-loud stories shared in the discussion:

> This story reminds me of my great-grandmother Ruth. In the story, the two children knew Death was coming soon for their beloved grandmother. It was sort of the same for Ruth. Every time the family was told something that happened to her, we were prepared. Soon enough, when the time came, she passed. We know she was losing her memory of people. We know she is happier where she is now. But back to the story, when their grandmother died, they looked out the window to remember her. To remember Ruth I will look out the window. I like to think of her amazing cooking.
> — WMS, Grade 5

> This story reminds me of the night when my dog Charlie died. Me and my sister were playing cards and every now and then we heard the cries of pain. My dad came downstairs and told us to walk to our friend's house while he took Charlie to the vet. We came home to find out that we lost a beloved family member and a great friend. Just like how the children pleaded Death not to kill their grandmother because they couldn't watch her die, me and my family felt the same. We were devastated for a year until we got a new dog. Her name is Katie.
> —ZL, Grade 4

> This story reminds me of the Greek Myth when Thantos, the God of Death, knocks on people's doors to get their signature for death. One person decides to cheat Death. The picture book reminds me of this myth because the kids didn't want their grandma to die. They didn't want to cheat Death but they learned that Joy goes with Sorrow and Delight goes with Grief.
> —AP, Grade 5

> When I listened to this story, I fondly remembered Jimmy, my old dog. He passed away about a year ago because he had cancer in this jaw. I wish i could have prevented this trajity (sic). I know that you can't have a pet forever, but the vet said it could either be a rotten tooth or cancer. I wish it was a rotten tooth. If it was, Jimmy might still be with us.
> —MR, Grade 5

> This story reminds me of Harry Potter because the character Death is like the Dementors in Harry Potter. Death and the Dementors look the same and they both have things to make people die. The Dementors guard a jail and suck souls. The Grim Reaper in this story brings people to death when he thinks they are ready.
> —KR, Grade 4

This story reminds me of my pet fish Mohock (sic). One time, he was sleeping and my dad flushed him down the toilet. He thought he was dead. Miss you Mohock.

— TS, Grade 5

Extensions

- Students can use the Internet to find more information about the Grim Reaper and/or how death is personified in different cultures.
- Other picture books about death (see Bookshelf on page 126) could be shared with students so they can consider how other authors have dealt with the sensitive issue, and perhaps be inspired to further grasp the meaning and universality of stories about death.

Boys Don't Wear Dresses: Considering and Respecting Gender Equity

If you see a Princess Boy...
  Will you laugh at him?
  Will you call him a name?
  Will you play with him?
  Will you like him for who he is?

— Cheryl Kilodavis, *My Princess Boy*

Raising My Rainbow: Adventures of Raising a Fabulous, Gender Creative Son is Lori Duron's account of the distress and happiness of raising a gender-nonconforming boy who happens to like girl stuff.

When speaking about books that are considered multicultural, it is important to consider books that deal with gender issues and sexual preferences along with books about race, ethnicity, disability, religion, and socioeconomic status. We need to be critical of the speech, language, physical appearances, and relationships among characters portrayed that are not considered stereotypical but are true to life. Do characters have unique personalities? Is there diversity within depicting gender behavior?

Gender equity is a way of thinking. Yes, boys and girls are different from each other. But the differences within any gender are greater than the differences between the two genders. What kind of boy? What kind of girl? For many reasons (e.g., brain differences; nurture and nature; peer and media influences), our students hold strong stereotypes for the activities their gender participates in. In the past decade, several books have celebrated children and young adolescents who are coming to terms, or have come to terms, with their gender identity. Such stories of "gender creative" youth need to be shared in order to help a community of learners consider their own values and to promote understanding and acceptance of those considered easy targets for taunting. Moreover, when they see themselves represented in multicultural literature, many students come to realize they're not alone. Exposing young and older students to stories in which the character's gender identity is different from his or her assigned birth gender, and encouraging all children to empathize with such a character's experience, encourages students to be accepting and shows them a path to living their truth without fear or shame.

Bookshelf: Books About Gender

Picture Books

Baldacchino, Christine; illus. Isabelle Malenfant. *Morris Micklewhite and the Tangerine Dress* (French: *Boris Brindamour et la robe orange*)
Cole, Babette. *Princess Smartypants*
dePaola, Tomie. *Oliver Button is a Sissy*
Ewert, Marcus; illus. Rex Ray. *10,000 Dresses*
Herthel, Jessica and Jazz Jennings; illus. Shelagh McNicholas. *I Am Jazz*

Hoffman, Sarah and Ian; illus. Chris Case. *Jacob's New Dress*
Kilodavis, Cheryl; illus. Suzanne DeSimone. *My Princess Boy*
Shraya, Vivek; illus. Rajini Perera. *The Boy & The Bindi*
Zolotow, Charlotte; illus. William Pene Du Bois. *William's Doll*

Novels: Middle Years

Cassidy, Sara. *A Boy Named Queen*
Gephart, Donna. *Lily and Dunkin*
Gino, Alex. *George*
Hennessey, M.G. *The Other Boy*
Howe, James. *Totally Joe*
Huser, Glen. *Stitches*
Walliams, David. *The Boy in the Dress*

Novels: Young Adult

Beam, Cris. *I am J*
Clark, Kristin Elizabeth. *Freakboy*
Peters, Julie Anne. *Luna*
Saenz, Benjamin Alire. *Aristotle and Dante Discover the Secrets of the Universe*
Williamson, Lisa. *The Art of Being Normal*
Wittlinger, Ellen. *Parrotfish*

THINKING STEMS

Guest Voice: David Sexsmith, Grade 3/4 Teacher

Thinking stems, or prompts, invite students to respond to a text in writing. Each prompt can connect to a comprehension strategy. The following two methods can be used when using Sentence Stems:

- Students can be assigned three different prompts to complete.
- Students can be offered a list of various prompts and they can choose which ones they want to respond to.

Thinking stems are a useful way to have students reflect on their reading and reveal their responses on paper. It is a convenient strategy for honoring individual, personal responses to a text where answers can be open-ended. Once thinking stems have been completed, students can work in groups of three or four to share their responses. The class, as a whole, can then have a discussion about the text, where different views are shared and listened to. Students can be given the opportunity to write a response to the story following a discussion where they've shared or listened to different opinions of the story.

Students can use the Thinking Stems sheet on page 133 to record their responses to a text they have listened to being read aloud, or one that they have read independently. Students can be assigned specific prompts to complete or they can complete the sheet using the following outline:

1. Students choose any three sentence stems to complete.
2. Students meet with a partner to share responses and discuss the text.
3. Students meet in groups of four and use the sentence stems that have not been filled in to discuss the text.

The sentence-stems strategy provided a meaningful response strategy for students in the class to share their reactions, emotional connections, and personal experiences in unpacking the issue of gender equity.

I believe *Morris Micklewhite and The Tangerine Dress* is an effective resource to support teaching about gender equity issues in the classroom. Morris is a character who fully embraces what he likes: wearing a tangerine dress, painting out-of-this world scenes, and going on imaginative adventures. In the story, Morris is not like the other boys in the classroom. Morris enjoys wearing the dress. He displays pink polish that his mother painted on his nails. He pretends he doesn't hear the putdowns of those in his classroom: "We don't want you to turn us into girls." As the story unfolds, it is the boys who come around to appreciate Morris's great imagination and see him for his positive qualities. The author ends the story on a self-affirming note: another character tries to shame Morris with "Boys don't wear dresses":

> Morris smiled as he swished, crinkled and clicked back to his spaceship.
> "This boy does!"

I wish I had a book like this on the bookshelf when I was in younger to help me understand that those who may seem flamboyant and "different" can be considered confident and proud, unique and strong. Moreover, in presenting picture books and novels with characters like Morris (see list on pages 129–130), I hope we are open enough as educators to encourage children to fully express their gender identities. Let us raise the next generation of children who won't have to go through the shame and self-hating that so many transgendered people and people with a more fluid gender identity have gone through.

Students were provided with a sheet with the following three sentence stem prompts:

> I feel…
> I remember/I am reminded of…
> I wonder…

Following the reading of *Morris Micklewhite and the Tangerine Dress*, students were given time to record their thoughts in reaction to the text. The written responses were used as a framework for a discussion about the book and about the issues of gender equity, bullying, and acceptance.

> *I feel…*
> … happy that he told Becky that he'd give back the dress when he's done with it.
> … happy that Morris stuck up for himself.
> … sad for Morris. No one can tell you what to do.
> … frustrated because this story is offensive to girls because girls aren't that mean.
> … my head is going to explode because people make fun of me.

> *I remember/I am reminded of…*
> … a book called *You're Mean, Lily Jean* about a girl who was excluded.
> … doing ballet when I was young. I wore a puffy dress and all the older kids made fun of me.

... the story The Emperor's New Clothes because people laughed at him.

... Martin Luther King Jr because he was black and his best friend was white and his dad didn't let Martin Luther Kng Jr. play with him.

I wonder...

... where the teacher was. Was she in the washroom? Prediction: Maybe she was just watching Morris because she wanted to see if he could solve problems by himself.

... why people bullied Morris because they didn't even know why he was wearing the dress.

... why didn't Morris just say, "Stop teasing me!!"

... what would I do if I was in Morris's class?

Thinking Stems

1. Choose three of the following sentence stems to record your response to a text you have read or listened to.
2. Once you have completed three stems, share and compare your responses with a partner who may have chosen three different items to reflect upon.
3. Meet in groups of four. Use sentence stems that have not been written about to reflect and discuss the text you have read or listened to.

I know…

I predict…

I like…

I don't like…

I feel…

I hope…

I imagine…

I remember…

I am reminded of…

I want to know more about…

I'm puzzled by…

I wonder…

Pembroke Publishers ©2017 *Take Me to Your Readers* by Larry Swartz ISBN 978-1-55138-326-2

Confronting the Bully Issue: Considering Healthy Relationships

If we are to raise kids who think and act ethically, we don't begin with the thinking or the acting. We begin with caring.
— Barbara Coloroso, *Just Because It's Not Wrong Doesn't Make It Right*

If I can stop one heart from breaking,
I shall not live in vain;
If I can ease one life the aching,
Or cool one pain,
Or help one fainting robin
Unto his nest again,
I shall not live in vain.

— Emily Dickinson

These two resources outline a range of strategies to help build an understanding of the bully issue: *The Bully-Go Round* by Larry Swartz and *Creating Caring Classrooms* by Kathleen Gould Lundy and Larry Swartz. Both outline how Community, Communication, Collaboration, and Compassion need to be addressed in any program in order to then confront the bully Issue.

The statistics are irrefutable.

The headlines are frightening.

The stories are painful.

With the increasing severity of bullying and the accompanying media attention that bullying cases have received, educators (and parents) have cause to take action and ensure that bullying does not go unnoticed. What, in fact, are schools doing to identify, understand, and confront problems with bullying? What procedures, policies, and programs are in place to acknowledge and address bullying? How do we help young people to live with integrity, civility, and compassion?

As educators, we feel a responsibility to introduce strategies that can help students come to understand those involved in the bully triangle: the bully, the bullied, and the bystander. Young people have the right to be free from teasing, harassment, and intimidation, and must feel safe, secure, accepted, and valued at school. We have to both help students understand why bullies behave the way they do and recognize that students who are bullies are capable of showing positive actions. We also need to provide students with strategies to use if they are caught in the bully web.

Bullying, according to researcher Debra Peplar, is a relationship problem and needs relationship solutions. In our classrooms, we need to create social contexts that promote positive interactions. We need to find space in the curriculum to help students understand that everyone has the right to respect. We also need to introduce stories in the media, novels, picture books, poetry, films, and YouTube selections that invite written, oral, and dramatic responses so that students can make connections and consider strategies for dealing with troublesome situations. Fiction and nonfiction sources can provide contexts in which educators can share ideas and respond to those around us. Each piece of literature we offer about bullying offers a case study of a situation that can help our students stand up for their own rights while respecting the rights and legitimate needs of others, to handle conflicts nonviolently, and to act with integrity when confronted with difficult situations.

Bookshelf: Books about Bullying

Picture Books

Agassi, Martine; illus. Marieka Heinlen. *Hands Are Not for Hitting*
Baldacchino, Christine; illus. Isabelle Malenfant. *Morris Micklewhite and the Tangerine Dress*
Browne, Anthony. *Willy the Champ.* (Also *Willy the Wimp; Willy and Hugh*)
Choi, Yangsook. *The Name Jar*
Mobin-Uddin, Asma; illus. Barbara Kiwak. *My Name is Bilal*
Moss, Peggy; illus. Lea Lyon. *Say Something*
Polacco, Patricia. *Bully* (Also *Mr. Lincoln's Way*)
Ross, Tony. *Is it Because?*
Seskin, Steve & Allen Shamblin; illus. Glin Dibley. *Don't Laugh At Me*
Wishinsky, Frieda; illus. Kady MacDonald Denton. *You're Mean, Lily Jean.*
Woodson, Jacqueline; illus. E. B. Lewis. *Each Kindness*

Novels

The Bully, The Bullied, The Bystander, The Brave by David Booth and Larry Swartz (eds) is a noteworthy collection of 65 poems centred on the complex issue of bullying.

Anderson, John David. *Posted*
Blume, Judy. *Blubber*
Clements, Andrew. *Jake Drake Bully Buster* (chapter book)
Gardner, Graham. *Inventing Elliot*
Hale, Shannon; illus. LeUyen Pham. *Real Friends*
Howe, James. *The Misfits*
Kerz, Anna. *Better Than Weird*
Nielsen, Susin. *The Reluctant Journal of Henry K. Larsen*
Palacio, R.J. *Wonder*

Paterson, Katherine. *The Field of the Dogs*
Patterson, James and Chris Grabenstein; illus. Stephen Gilpin. *Pottymouth and Stoopid*
Pignat, Caroline. *Egghead*
Preller, James. *Bystander*
Sher, Emil. *Young Man With Camera*
Singer, Nicky. *Feather Boy*
Spinelli, Jerry. *Loser* (Also *Wringer*)
Wolk, Lauren. *Wolf Hollow*

📚 FINDING A DEFINITION OF BULLYING

Larry visits Diane Chieco's Grade 5 Classroom

> *Bullying is a relationship problem in which power and aggression are used to cause distress to a vulnerable person.*
> — Wendie M. Craig and Debra J. Pepler, Professors of Psychology

It is important to consider how bullying is different from other areas of conflict. By putting the students in the role of dictionary editors to define the concept of bully, they can come to choose vocabulary that they think is relevant and are challenged to articulate the behaviors inherent in bullying situations.

The following instructions guided students through the process of defining *bully* as they worked independently, in pairs, in small groups, and as a whole class.

1. Introduce the activity:

   A new dictionary is about to be published, but the word bully has yet to be defined. As dictionary editors, you have been called upon for input.

2. To begin students work independently. Each student is given a file card on which to write a personal definition of the word *bully* as a noun or as a verb. There are no restrictions to word length.
3. Students work in pairs to exchange definitions. Ask students to consider this question: "What words or phrases from your partner's definition do you think you might like to borrow to include in a definition of bully?" These suggestions can be recorded on a chart displayed to the whole group.
4. Pairs work together to synthesize definitions. Encourage students to include words from each partner's definition as well as add new words.
5. Partners are matched up with others to share definitions. In groups of four, students collaborate on a definition. Challenge students by insisting that the new definition be exactly 22 words (or another number of your choice) in length. Once definitions are completed, one member of each group shares the definition with the whole class.
6. A shared writing activity with the students is implemented to arrive at a class definition of the word *bully*. Each suggestion that is offered is recorded. The definition is revised and edited as the composing process unfolds.
7. Inform students that the new dictionary will be strictly visual, so all definitions must be represented without words. Prompt students to create an image or design to represent what a bully or bullying is.

Extensions

- Students examine definitions from a dictionary or the Internet to compare with their own.
- Share Barbara Coloroso's definition with students. What words from student definitions are similar to Coloroso's? How might they alter Coloroso's definition?

   Bullying is a conscious, willful and deliberate hostile activity intended to harm, induce fear through the threat of further aggression and create terror.
   — Barbara Coloroso, *The Bully, The Bullied, The Bystander* (2002, p. 13)

When asked in an interview how she might alter her original definition, Coloroso offered the following, adapted from the picture book *Don't Laugh At Me*:

A bully is a person who gets pleasure from someone else's pain.

Samples of Student Responses

A bully is:

… an unkind person who is unhappy about themselves. He or she bullies weaker people to give themselves more power.

… an insecure person who is leads a group of people to attack others physically, verbally or on Social Media.

… a person who feels sad and wants to make everyone feel like that. Bullies seek power by overpowering others.

… a mean person who might feel jealous of someone else so they tease, taught or target him (or her).

Toward an Understanding of Poverty: Building Compassion, Empathy, and Awareness of Social Issues

It's easier to look the other way. But if you do, terrible things can happen.

— Eve Bunting, *Fly Away Home*

Every day Chloe would pass Mr. Stink and his dog in her parents' car on the way to her posh private school. Millions of thoughts and questions would swim through her head. Who was he? Why did he live on the streets? Had he ever had a home? What did is dog eat? Did he have any friends or family? If so did they know he was homeless?"

— David Walliams, *Mr. Stink*

With thanks to Jim Giles, manager of the Poverty Project, ETFO.

Possibilities: Addressing Poverty in Elementary Schools from the Elementary Teachers' Federation of Ontario (ETFO) is a comprehensive teacher resource book designed not only to encourage educators to understand tensions, assumptions, and biases they may unknowingly hold but also to take action.

The gap between rich and poor continues to widen in North America. One in five children in Canada now live in poverty—that's about 3 million children. (Campaign 2000, 2016). In fact, Canada's income gap is among the fastest growing in the developed world and is the result of a myriad of political and social reasons, including the decline of unions (OECD report, 2016).

Eradicating child poverty is a complex issue! Schools are affected by the circumstances in which children grow up, including the negativity that is often associated with the poor. Poverty continues to be the single highest predictor of student achievement, well-being, and life outcomes. Educators in every school face issues of poverty in some way or another, while we all want every student to reach their full potential. To do this, educators must resist and critique "deficit frameworks" of poverty to better understand the contexts in which students and families can live, learn, and thrive.

Schools and educators can contribute in an important way to alleviating the effects of poverty and inequities by finding a place in the curriculum to present material that ignites awareness and reflection of the complex issue of poverty. Children's literature is a powerful vehicle for understanding cultures and experiences of others that differ from your own. Literature that is centred on poverty issues can promote social awareness through a variety of themes and contexts, such as basic needs, caring for others, diversity, depictions of economic challenges, and homelessness. Presenting these stories in the classroom can help educators and their students challenge assumptions and stereotypes about people living in poverty. Fiction and nonfiction resources are able to evoke debate and social awareness and arouse critical thinking and emotions to challenge preconceived beliefs related to poverty. Children's literature is a "safe" place for students to explore the stories and impact of poverty on others, while also inviting them to unpack any personal connections to the issue that they may choose to reveal.

Tableaux depict a moment in time. Students can represent a story by creating images in different periods of time and present two or more images sequentially. Presenting a series of tableaux is a convenient way to retell story events: three to five images can be used to represent the beginning, middle, climax, and ending of the story. When instructed to show scenes that might not be in the story, students are moving beyond retelling by considering possibilities and abstract ideas inherent in the story. Since creating tableaux encourages—indeed, requires—students to represent ideas nonverbally, this dramatic form helps students succinctly represent explicit and implicit events. When teachers choose to introduce this drama convention, they are providing students with an active, physical response that encourages them to demonstrate comprehension by considering the main ideas of the story (what happens in the story); the sequence of events (the beginning, middle, and end of the story); making predictions (what you think happened in the past/what you think will happen in the future); and making inferences (what scene might not be in the story but could be/ what the character might be thinking about or dreaming).

Bookshelf: Books about Poverty

Picture Books

Boelts, Maribeth; illus Noah Z. Jones. *Those Shoes*
Bunting, Eve; illus. Ronald Himler. *Fly Away Home*
De La Peña, Matt; illus. Christian Robinson. *Last Stop on Market Street*
Estes, Eleanor; illus. Louis Slobodkin. *The Hundred Dresses*
Garay, Luis. *The Kite*
Gunning, Monica; illus. Elaine Pedlar. *A Shelter in Our Car*
Hathorn, Libby. *Way Home*
Mills, Lauren. *The Rag Coat*
McGovern, Ann; illus. Marni Backer. *The Lady in the Box*
McPhail, David. *The Teddy Bear*
Rylant, Cynthia; illus. Peter Catalanotto. *An Angel For Solomon Singer*
Wild, Margaret; illus. Anne Spudvilas. *Woolvs in the Sitee*
Williams, Vera B. *A Chair for My Mother*
Woodson, Jacqueline; illus. E.B. Lewis. *Each Kindness*
Wyeth, Sharon Dennis; illus. Chris K. Soentpiet. *Something Beautiful*

Novels

Applegate, Katherine. *Crenshaw*
D'Adamo, Francesco. *Iqbal: A novel*
DiCamillo, Kate; illus. Yoko Tanaka. *The Magician's Elephant*
Little, Jean. *Willow and Twig*
Nielsen, Susin. *Word Nerd*
O'Connor, Barbara. *How to Steal a Dog*
Pinkney, Andrea Davis; illus. Shane W. Evans. *The Red Pencil*
Ryan, Pam Muñoz. *Esperanza Rising*
Walliams, David. *Mr. Stink*
Walters, Eric. *Shattered.*

Script

Craig, David S. *Danny, King of the Basement*

In *Those Shoes* by Maribeth Boelts, more than anything, Jeremy wants to own a pair of shoes that everyone in his school seems be wearing, and although his grandmother would love to grant Jeremy his wishes, she can't really afford to buy the shoes her grandson wants. Besides, what Jeremy really needs is a pair of new winter boots.

TABLEAUX

Guest Voice: Steve Lieberman, Occasional Teacher, Grade 3

In tableaux, students are invited to create still images using their bodies to crystallize a moment or an idea drawn from a story, a theme, or an abstract idea. By creating a frozen picture alone or with others, students are required to discuss, negotiate, and make a decision on images that will communicate or represent ideas. When students are audiences for tableaux, they are encouraged to brainstorm the range of messages that may be contained within a single image.

The following outlines the steps that invited students to create tableaux images connected to the picture book, *Those Shoes* by Maribeth Boelts:

Tableau #1: Creating an Image to Accompany Text

1. To introduce the story, I covered the book so students couldn't see the title and cover art. I then read the first four sentences of the story without showing the illustrations.

   > I have dreams about those shoes.
   > Black high-tops.
   > Two white stripes.
   > "Grandma, I want them."

2. I then had students select a partner and together show the scene where the child is speaking with his grandma in the form of a tableau or frozen picture. As a follow-up, volunteer pairs shared their work with the class. The audience responded to the tableau images by commenting on the story, the relationships, and the feelings of the characters.

3. Students were reminded of some criteria for an effective tableau to help them repeat the activity by revising their initial tableau image:

   > Is there a focal point to draw an audience's attention to what is happening?
   > Is there use of levels (high, medium, low) to make the image interesting?
   > How does posture, gesture, facial expression help bring meaning to the images?

4. Collective role playing with dialogue: The partners were separated, with one group made up of the students who were the grandchild in the tableaux and the other being the grandma. The group with the grandchildren was secretly told that they would re-create their tableaux, but would be able to talk to the grandma character, who could then answer, thus creating a dialogue. Their first line was to be "Grandma, I want them…" This group was given a few minutes to think about how they would convince Grandma to buy the desired shoes. While they were contemplating this, I approached the second group and explained that their grandchild was going to try and convince them to buy the shoes, but that they couldn't afford them. One of their lines in the forthcoming

dialogue was to be, "There's no room for 'want' around here—just 'need.'" This group was then given a few minutes to think about their line and how they would respond to their grandchild.

Tableau #2: From Still Image to Improvisation

1. The partners were reunited and re-created their original tableaux. The grandchild began with "Grandma, I want them…" to start the dialogue. The conversations continued for less than two minutes.
2. On a signal, students froze into a tableau that depicted the boy and his grandmother at some point in the conversation. Volunteer groups shared their presentations, beginning with a tableau that then came to life for a conversation, and ending with a tableau.
3. When they had completed this re-creation, students reflected on what they saw and heard. Bribery and full-out tantrums were used to try to convince Grandma, while dejection, disappointment, and sadness were clearly observed in both characters when it was evident that the shoes were not going to be bought.

Tableau #3: Retelling the Story

1. After listening to the story, students worked in groups of four to retell the significant events of *Those Shoes* in three frozen images. Each image would represent the beginning, middle, or conclusion of the story. Students were asked to consider: Who would be in the scene? What was taking place? How would the characters' feelings be represented in each tableau?
2. Students were given time to rehearse the story. A drum was used as a signal to help students transition from one scene to the next. Groups were partnered to compare how they each told the story in tableaux.

Attention Must Be Paid:
Building Insight, Understanding, and Inquiry into
First Nations, Métis, and Inuit Cultures

*The truths that Truth and Reconciliation Commission unveiled about
residential schooling will not bring reconciliation without education.*

— Justice Murray Sinclair, Chairman of the Truth
and Reconciliation Commission

With thanks to Nancy Steele, Project Manager, Deepening Knowledge: Resources for and about Aboriginal Education, Ontario Institute for Studies in Education, and to John Doran, OISE instructor and First Nation member.

Dr. John Doran, Mi'Kmaq, Schubenacadie First Nation, Pipe Carrier for his nation, asks all settler Canadians to realize

You are on Indigenous land; you have a responsibility to know about it. You have responsibilities through still-relevant and valid treaties with the Indigenous peoples of this land. Everyone living on Turtle Island needs to know this. Indigenous people are not part of the multicultural movement. They were the first humans here. Indigenous peoples have unique legal agreements with the Canadian government, land and Settlers. These agreements need to be taught in schools. Attempts to destroy the cultures and assimilate the Indigenous Peoples including Residential Schools have shaken the Indigenous world to the core, and have done almost irreparable damage. This history must also be taught.

But many teachers worry about teaching this history: Since I know so little myself, will I offend when I try to teach about it? Families who identify as Indigenous today represent just over 4% of the population of Canada. How can I meet the needs of all my other students and the demands of the ministry for changes in pedagogy and, at the same time, do justice to this task? How will I deal with comments that seem stereotypical and racial that might emerge in discussions of this content?

Education delving into issues needs to start in our classrooms. All Canadian children need to know that Indigenous cultures at the time of first European contact were complex and sophisticated. The importance of many of the values and understandings of these cultures are only now being generally recognized, as people in the dominant culture begin to appreciate environmental sustainability and the benefits of restorative rather than punitive justice. It is essential that teachers receive help both in learning about this missing history and in finding resources they can use with all children to teach about it respectfully.

RAISING QUESTIONS

Guest Voice: Monique Pregent

One of the recommendations from the Truth and Reconciliation Commission is that the education system become a vehicle to help educate Canadians about the true Canadian history that involved residential schools, and about how Indigenous culture has been affected by it. This would be a big step toward reconciliation, and toward ensuring that Indigenous culture is present in every classroom—a task that could easily be done by incorporating Indigenous culture into the pedagogy of our subjects. Children's literature can be a significant vehicle for bringing Indigenous culture into the classroom, for paying attention to authentic Indigenous voices, and to initiate the reading of fiction and nonfiction resources that lead to further investigation. Young people learn largely through inquiry. Having students ask probing questions about what they are reading helps them develop an understanding that stems from their own curiosity. Having them come up with questions from reading books that have Indigenous content encourages the avidity to learn more about Indigenous culture.

In Indigenous cultures, stories have historically been shared orally. Until recent years, many books with Indigenous content were committed to paper with biases and inaccuracies. There are now a large number of excellent books in print that come from an Indigenous perspective, as well as books written by Indigenous authors that can be used in the classroom in the study of all subjects.

When we read, we often become curious about what is happening, what might happen, and what will happen. These questions, or puzzlements or wonderings, can spur us on to continue reading. As a comprehension strategy, questions can prompt our reading before, during, and after we finish a book. Questions can stimulate the minds of students, helping them go beyond what they know. When questions are raised by either teacher or students, it promotes a sense of inquiry, the urge to find out something or reveal inside-the-head thoughts and curiosities. Questions help build wonder at the same time as inviting students to seek information, to consider possibilities.

Bookshelf: Books Centred on Indigenous Voices and Culture

Picture Books, Biography, Legends

Alexie, Sherman; illus. Yuyi Morales. *Thunder Boy Jr.*
Bouchard, David. *The Song Within My Heart* (Also *The Drum Calls Softly; Nokum Is My Teacher; The Secret of Your Name*)
Brown, Chester. *Louis Riel: A Comic-Strip Biography*
Campbell, Nicola; illus. Kim LaFave. *Shi-Shi-Etko* (Also *Shin-chi's Canoe*)
Currie, Susan. *The Mask That Sang*
Daniel, Danielle. *Sometimes I Feel Like a Fox*
Eyvindsen, Peter; illus. Sheldon Dawson. *Kookum's Red Shoes*
Florence, Melanie; illus. Gabrielle Grimard. *Stolen Words*
Florence, Melanie; illus. François Thisdale. *Missing Nimâmâ*
Joe, Saqamaw Mi'Sel; illus. Clara Dunn. *Muinji'j Becomes a Man*
Jordan-Fenton, Christy & Margaret Pokiak-Fenton; illus. Gabrielle Grimard. *When I Was Eight* (Also *Not My Girl*)

Neering, Rosemary. *Louis Riel*
Robertson, Joanne. *The Water Walker*
Simpson, Caroll. *Brothers of the Wolf* (Also *The First Beaver; The First Mosquito; The Salmon Twins*)
Slipperjack, Ruby. *Little Voice*
Sprung, Dawn; illus. Charles Bullshields. *The Legend of the Buffalo Stone*
Stellings, Caroline. *The Contest*
van Keuren, L. W. *Raven, Stay by Me*

Nonfiction

Ipellie, Alootook with David MacDonald. *The Inuit Thought of It: Amazing Arctic Innovations*
Sigafus, Kim and Lyle Ernst. *Wisdom From Our First Nations*
Wallace, Mary. *An Inuksuk Means Welcome*
Wilson, Janet. *Shannen and the Dream for a School*

Series

The First Nations Series for Young Readers (Second Story Press)
Turtle Island Voices (Rubicon Publishers)

Young Adult

Bouchard, David; paintings by Dennis J. Weber. *Proud to be Métis*
Charleyboy, Lisa and Mary Beth Leatherdale (eds.) *Dreaming in Indian*
Coates, Ken. *#Idlenomore and the Remaking of Canada*
Downie, Gord; illus. Jeff Lemire. *Secret Path*
Nelson, Colleen. *250 Hours*
Ratt, Solomon. *Wood Cree Stories*
Saigeon, Lori. *Fight For Justice*
Watetch, Abel. *Payepot and His People*
White, Tara. *Where I Belong*

For more on questioning, see
- Koechlin, Carol and Sandi Zwann (2006) *Q Tasks*.
- Morgan, Norah and Juliana Saxton (2006) *Asking Better Questions*.

Using the sources listed, inquiry was ignited by questions raised by students.

Métis Culture and History

Book: *Louis Riel* by Rosemary Neering (Series: The Canadians)

Inquiry/Key Questions

- How was Louis Riel a heroic victim for Métis rights and culture?
- Was Riel a Canadian hero?
- Why has Louis Riel been considered an outlaw?
- How was Riel considered a divinely chosen leader and prophet?
- What led Prime Minister MacDonald to hang Louis Riel?

This title was shared as a read-aloud with Grade 8 students. As the students listened to the book, I was able to clarify the cause of events and the historical impact. The read-aloud experience allowed me to discuss events in detail and receive questions from the students to help clarify understanding. Questions emerged that led to further inquiry into the life of Riel and provided a context for further online and print resources.

Ojibway Culture and History

Source: *The Birchbark House* by Louise Erdrich (The Birchbark series)

Inquiry/Key Questions

- In what ways was birchbark vital to the Ojibway community?
- What is smallpox? Its cause? Its prevention? Is it always fatal?
- Why might someone intentionally infect the Aboriginal community with a deadly virus?
- How is community vital to the Aboriginal tribe?

The Birchbark House is the first of four books in a series known as The Birchbark series, which follows the life of Omakayas ("little frog") and her Ojibway community from 1847 to the present day. Framed by the four seasons, the first story describes Omakayas' connection to nature and the discovery of her gift of dreams. The novel is important for providing information regarding Ojibway cultural practices. Reading this book aloud to Grade 6 students provided me with the opportunity to integrate learning that covered both social studies and language arts. The book provided me with the opportunity to consider narrative features of a text, including the main idea, sequencing of events, and making inferences about Indigenous life. Since birchbark was important to the story, the class considered how this natural resource was important to Indigenous people. Métis elder Marcel Labelle was invited into the class to teach a lesson on birchbark canoes and students had the opportunity to create their own canoe models.

The book describes how members of Omokayas's family died from smallpox. It raised many inquiry questions:

- What was smallpox?
- How might it have been prevented?
- What are the treatments?
- Why didn't Omokayas get struck by smallpox when nearly everyone in the community did?

I invited one group to research how settlers were responsible for the smallpox crisis among Indigenous peoples, which included an inquiry into the practice of using smallpox-laden blankets as gifts to help kill off Indigenous people. Further research into contagious viruses also supported science-related investigations.

📖 INQUIRY INTO RESIDENTIAL SCHOOLS

Guest Voice: Monique Pregent

Open-ended questions can serve a variety of functions, including introducing reading tasks by stimulating interest and curiosity, setting up problems that require careful reading, identifying important ideas to look for when reading, and helping readers to construct meaning and initiate dialogue with others. Good questions

- Promote discussion, allowing a give and take of ideas

- Provide a purpose for our reading, helping us to focus on what the author (and/or illustrator) has said (and/or shown)
- Challenge our existing thinking, encouraging reflection

To further enrich the questioning experience, a Question Matrix can be used as a vehicle to help teachers (and students) consider questions that help look inside and outside a text. Depending on the language we use, questions can help readers move to deeper, more critical thinking about stories they have heard or read. See page 147 for the Question Matrix.

Students can be divided into groups, with each group given a resource to respond to. Students use the Question Matrix and work collaboratively to record questions before, during, and after reading the story.

Sample Questions

- What might some benefits be to those who attended Residential Schools?
- When were you able to tell the story of your experiences for the first time?
- Which was your worst memory or memories?
- Who would protect the students at Residential Schools?
- Why were students given numbers and not names?
- Why would families let their children be taken to Residential Schools and not fight to keep them?
- How did you hope?
- How will Aboriginal people recover from this history?
- How would Reconciliation be meaningful?
- How might Indigenous Peoples get their culture back?

Booklist: The Residential School Experience

Campbell, Nicola; illus. Kim LaFave. *Shi-shi-etko* (Also *Shin-chi's Canoe*)

Downie, Gord; illus. Jeff Lemire. *Secret Path*

Eyvindsen, Peter. *Kookum's Red Shoes*

Florence, Melanie; illus. Gabrielle Grimard. *Stolen Words*

Jordan-Fenton, Christy and Margaret Pokiak-Fenton; illus. Gabrielle Grimard. *When I Was Eight* (Also *Not My Girl*)

Jordan-Fenton, Christy and Margaret Pokiak-Fenton; illus. Liz Amini-Holmes. *Fatty Legs* (Also *A Stranger at Home*)

Loyie, Larry; illus. Heather Holmlund. *As Long As the Rivers Flow*

Question Matrix

	Who	What	Where	When	Why	How
is						
did						
can						
might						
would						
will						

Pembroke Publishers ©2017 *Take Me to Your Readers* by Larry Swartz ISBN 978-1-55138-326-2

5

Connected To Curriculum

Integrating themes and topics, within and across subjects, are some ways that teachers can conquer a crowded curriculum. Teachers look for and then take up the threads in the very busy tapestry called the curriculum.

— Kathleen Gould Lundy, *Conquering the Crowded Curriculum*

Curriculum is whatever a student is doing at any particular moment in time.

— Richard Courtney

One afternoon, a group of teacher candidates visited my office to ask advice about books to use in their teaching: "Have you got a picture book about electricity?" "Are there books about the different food groups, particularly grains and rice?" "How can I use a picture book to teach about body parts?" I had done such a good job motivating my students to use children's literature in their teaching that they were eager to challenge me to provide titles to support their lesson planning in a number of curriculum areas. With the use of the Internet, it is likely we can find a book to match most units explored outside of language arts. What I had yet to help teaching students to understand (as I myself slowly came to understand) is that most fiction that we share in our classrooms provides information to help broaden students' knowledge and understanding of the world.

Language skills are at the centre of learning in all subject areas. We need to ensure that our students have sufficient opportunities to explore a subject from multiple perspectives by giving careful consideration to cross-curricular learning and integrated learning. All content subjects, including the arts, require that students communicate what they have learned both orally and in writing. Math, science, technology, social studies, health and physical education, and certainly media studies provide contexts for students to develop literacy skills and provide them with authentic purposes for reading, writing, listening, speaking, viewing, and representing. Each discipline has expectations that are unique but, when integrating learning, we can provide students with multiple opportunities to demonstrate their knowledge and skills.

We may tend to think of nonfiction resources as the go-to genre when exploring such topics as animal habitats, electricity, ancient civilizations, healthy bodies, etc., but many picture books and novels can support and provide background for cross-curricular studies. In this chapter, several booklists are provided to help you consider cross-curricular learning. Also suggested are response strategies that include reading, writing, technology, and media as opportunities for using language to respond creatively and critically to a text—no matter what the subject.

For Your Consideration

- ☐ How do you promote effective reading in the content subjects (i.e., math, science, social studies, health, the arts)?
- ☐ How successfully do you include fiction and nonfiction when teaching content subjects?
- ☐ What does integration mean to you in planning your literacy program?
- ☐ How is writing a part of your reading program?
- ☐ What consideration is given to genre study in connecting to the curriculum subjects?
- ☐ In what ways does your reading program connect to technology and digital learning?
- ☐ How successfully do you use inquiry as a model for language growth?
- ☐ How does the library support your planning and implementation of curriculum units?
- ☐ Agree or Disagree: Using children's literature when teaching different subjects is important.
- ☐ What does this statement mean to you? *Every book students read (or listen to) is the curriculum.*

Math + Literacy = Literacy + Math:
When Readers Read, Write, and Talk in Math Class

A version of this article was published in *Speaking of Reading* Newsletter, Reading For the Love Of It, Spring 2017. With thanks.

David Booth, in his book *I've Got Something to Say* (2013), explains that "when we are dealing with new ideas or coming to new understandings, talk helps us make sense of both our thoughts and feelings. We need to tempt students into having 'something to say.'"

Separately and together, literacy and numeracy call upon the ability to use language, images, and representations in rich and varied forms to read, write, listen, speak, view, represent, and think critically about ideas. Both literacy and mathematics teachers need to teach their students to read and interpret and engage meaningfully with verbal and nonverbal text that includes pragmatics, vocabulary, information, story, and, in the case of mathematics, symbols, models, and numbers. Students can respond to texts through writing or the arts but, for both literacy and mathematics, it is essentially talk that provides the medium that encourages students to share their thinking with others as they work toward an understanding of information and problems.

Oral language and communication may be central to the language-arts curriculum, but talk as a learning medium is cross-curricular and vitally significant to learning in classrooms that are interactive and collaborative. Talk is not a subject; rather it is a condition for learning in all subjects. Rich, open-ended tasks in mathematics provide meaningful opportunities for exploratory talk that involves hypothesizing, questioning, and discovering.

In our classrooms, we need to create meaningful learning contexts in which each student's voice matters and where students can explore and apply language to think, to express, and to reflect upon ideas. If our goal is to help our students become skilled critical thinkers, thoughtful problem-solvers, and reflective communicators, educators need to

> ...strive to create a connected classroom culture that is built on trust and mutual respect, and where students are able to ask questions, pose problems, explore ideas and make informed decisions. (Fiore and Lebar, 2016, p. 9)

In reading programs, students are invited to read and respond to a wide range of texts that may include fiction, nonfiction, media, and poetry. In math class, students are invited to discuss mathematical texts using models, numbers, and mathematical symbols to represent their understanding. In both literacy and numeracy, students are called upon to activate prior knowledge and experience, to wonder, to analyze, to evaluate and synthesize information, and to make connections to their own lives and the world around them. In both literacy and numeracy, students are called upon to communicate their knowledge and understandings through writing and/or talk (talk can precede the writing; writing can precede talk). All communication is related to thinking. It is nuanced. It is connected to our ability to be critical about what we are thinking, saying, or hearing.

Good communicators are flexible. If they cannot explain it one way, they try another way. Consider these questions:

- Why do I think about this?
- Does this make sense?
- Will my explanation help others understand my thinking?

- Can I model/communicate this in a different way?
- Can I think effectively?
- Can I shift my thinking and communicate differently?

When students demonstrate an increased comfort level in talking about mathematical ideas, they demonstrate an out-loud understanding of mathematical concepts. Math talk promotes metacognition, which is thinking about one's own thinking. It enables students to assess their own mathematical ideas and those of others. Sharing through math talk helps students understand that there can be different mathematical solutions and strategies for one problem. By listening carefully to student talk in mathematics, teachers can assess student thinking and identify possible misconceptions students might have. Using visuals and manipulatives to facilitate math talk is critical, as this enables students to make strong connections between the math language they are using and the mathematical concepts they are exploring. Posing open questions, such as *Does that make mathematic sense? How do you know?* or *Can you show this in a different way?* invites rich mathematical discussions and sharing. Life is full of problems. To help solve our problems we have always been encouraged to talk about them. Mathematics is, amongst other things, about learning to solve problems. For sure, this is something to talk about.

Any discussion of math and literacy connections likely considers the world of picture books, which can be excellent resources for exploring mathematical images, concepts, and story. Picture books invite students to respond through talk and explore concepts central to the source. The rich illustrations in math picture books can help students improve their visualization of mathematics and enrich their mathematics vocabulary. Many picture books are ideal resources for inviting problem-solving and developing a deep understanding of math as they present mathematical concepts embedded in a story presented by the author. A range of picture books recently published allow students to discuss mathematical ideas in a storyline represented in symbols, words, and pictures.

Bookshelf: Picture books that Promote Math Talk

Of special note too, is the Math Readers series of 75+ award-winning leveled readers for emergent, early, and fluent readers, published by Rubicon Publishers. Each book in the series presents narrative and/or visual text that highlights a mathematical concept for students to respond to. Suggested activities for parents and teacher are provided to help explore concepts with young children.

Barnett, Mac; illus Jon Klassen. *Triangle* (geometric shapes)

Booth, Jack (ed.) *Math Readers* (series) (various concepts)

Hulme, Joy; illus Carol Schwartz. *Wild Fibonacci* (number sense)

Fromental, Jean-Luc; illus. Joëlle Jolivet. *365 Penguins* (number sense)

Hall, Michael. *Perfect Square* (geometry)

Jocelyn, Marthe. *Sam Sorts* (sorting and classifying)

Lazar, Tara; illus. Ross MacDonald. *7 Ate 9* (number sense)

McElligott, Matthew. *The Lion's Share: a tale of halving cake and eating it too* (multiplication)

Oxley, Jennifer and Billy Aronson. *Peg + Cat: The Pizza Problem* (series) (problem-solving)

Rosenthal, Amy Krouse; illus. Tom Lichtenheld. *Friendshape* (geometric shapes)

Scieszka, Jon; illus. Lane Smith. *Math Curse* (problem-solving)

Slate, Joseph; illus. Ashley Wolff. *Miss Bindergarten Celebrates the 100th Day of Kindergarten* (number sense)

Smith, David J.; illus. Steve Adams. *If... A mind bending way of looking at big ideas and numbers* (number sense)

Winters, Kari-Lynn; illus. Lori Sherritt-Fleming. *Hungry for Math: Poems to munch on* (various concepts)

Young, Cybèle. *Nancy Knows* (sorting and classification)

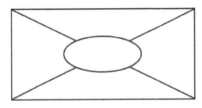

GRAPHIC ORGANIZER PLACEMATS

Guest Voice: Cathy Marks Krpan visits Marlene's Grade 3 Classroom

A placemat is a graphic organizer that provides a cooperative learning structure inviting students to reflect on their own thinking before sharing with others. For a group of four students, a piece of chart paper is divided into 4 sections, with a rectangle in the middle (see Placemat template in margin). In response to literature, students use the sections to respond to a specific question or prompt that connects them to the text. In mathematics, students work on a specific problem or question in their own space and then share their ideas with the group. Then, based on what each group member has shared, the group decides on a final answer and records it in the middle rectangle. This approach enables students to gain insight not only into other ways of thinking, but also into how others communicate their thinking using writing, mathematical symbols, and diagrams. This approach also enables all students to have a voice, as everyone has an opportunity to share and a physical place to record their thinking.

The placemat strategy also engages students in various forms of argumentation and debate as they determine which strategy is the most effective. In addition, individual student contributions, noted in each of the four sections around the central rectangle, allows us to see the ideas of each student in addition to the final solution recorded in the middle rectangle.

The following placemat activity was implemented in a Grade 3 classroom and outlines how the strategy helped the classroom teacher critically explore mathematical ideas with her students.

Nancy Knows by Cybèle Young was the winner of the Marilyn Baillie Picture book prize in 2016. The author has composed intricate paper sculptures that are assembled into an outline drawing of the main character, Nancy the elephant. Nancy remembers many things in an number of ways (e.g., by color, by shape, by function).

1. Marlene read the book *Nancy Knows* by Cybèle Young, aloud to her class. The images that appear throughout the book provided rich opportunities to discuss and explore the mathematical concepts of sorting and classification. On each page, we see different ways that Nancy the Elephant organizes a potpourri of small objects to help her remember them.

2. After reading the book aloud and investigating the different ways that Nancy sorted different sets of objects, Marlene arranged her students in groups of four and provided each group with a variety of objects and a piece of chart paper divided up into a placemat organizer. Marlene invited each group to sort the objects in as many different ways as possible. In their own section of their placemat, students used writing, images, and numbers to communicate the different ways they felt the objects could be classified and organized and the reasons for their choice.

3. Once they completed their placemat sections, students shared what they wrote with their group, often using the actual objects to model their ideas. Marlene noted that students used rich mathematical language to describe their ideas and to support their reasoning. Once everyone had an opportunity to share their ideas, each group was asked to determine which classification strategy they wanted to use as their final answer. They recorded their solution in the middle rectangle of the placemat. Marlene invited each group to share their final solutions with the whole class. As a final reflection, Marlene invited each group to compare their strategies to the ones Nancy the Elephant used.

Just the Facts
Integrating Literacy, Literature, and Science

When reading nonfiction texts connected to science topics, students use a somewhat different set of skills than they do when reading fiction. There is often a vocabulary and terminology that are unique to science and technology, and students are required to identify and interpret text features such as headings, labels, charts, and diagrams that present science and technology information in nonfiction selections, the Internet, and textbooks. We need to model and teach the strategies that support learning to read while students are reading to learn.

When teaching a thematic or curriculum unit, many teachers are keen to seek out resources from the library to support the program. Though informational texts predominate to support each strand of the science and technology curriculum, there may not be a quality example of children's fiction for each topic. There are bookshelves filled with literature connected to the lives of animals and plants for teaching life systems in the elementary grades, and we need to acknowledge that every fictional text is also a piece of nonfiction. Reading a fictional story about an animal is an ideal way to learn about an animal's characteristics and behaviors. When learning about characteristics of living things, growth in animals, and habitats, children's literature is a significant vehicle for activating prior knowledge, identifying important information, and stimulating inquiry into living things.

KWL STICKY NOTES

Larry visits Anita Myler's Grade 2 Classroom

KWL has become a popular instructional strategy that helps students combine new information with background knowledge. The process helps students develop technical vocabulary connected to a related topic. There is no one way to introduce the strategy, but traditionally three columns are provided as a graphic organizer for students to fill out independently or in pairs, or as a chart on display in front of the class where the teacher acts as a scribe to list

1. What We **K**now (activating prior knowledge)
2. What We **W**ant to Learn (questions)
3. What We **L**earned (research)

Ideally, the strategy should span a thematic unit over time. The chart can be incorporated before, during, and after a unit. KWL demonstrates to students that they are a community that can share information about a topic and also provides a forum that builds curiosity and inquiry.

The students in the Grade 2 class were embarking on a project on Growth and Changes in Animals. They had each chosen an animal they wished to investigate and had begun to gather books from the library to support their research.

I introduced students to a variation on the KWL model, invited them to share information they knew about penguins, and challenged them, as a class, to list 100 facts about penguins within a one-hour period.

Phase One: What Do We Know?

Yellow Sticky Notes

- Students worked independently. Each was given three yellow sticky notes. They were challenged to write three *different* facts, one for each note.
- In pairs, students shared information with three or four classmates. If two students wrote the same fact, one was asked to put the fact aside so that there wouldn't be repetition.
- Students each read one fact aloud and it was posted on a display board. An attempt was made to organize facts into categories (*Description*, *Behaviors*, *Food*). A fourth category emerged under *Other Facts*.

Phase Two: What Did We Learn from a Story?

Orange Sticky Notes

- The picture book *Penguin Problems* by Jory John was read aloud to the class. In this amusing book, a complaining penguin is trying to fit in and cope with the daily routines of living in Antarctica.
- Following the reading, students were asked to identify any new information they learned about penguins after listening to the story, and from a discussion. Written on orange sticky notes, they were displayed separately from the yellow ones on the board.

Phase Three: What Did We Learn from Research?

Green Sticky Notes

- Students worked with a partner, and each pair was given a nonfiction selection or information from the Internet. Each pair was to provide at least three new facts about penguins. Each fact was to be written on a green sticky note. There was a ten-minute time limit for this activity.
- The children shouted, "Hooray!" when 100 sticky notes were displayed on the wall. Sophia, Nickolas, and Jonathan were eager to add to the list and eagerly provided a batch of additional facts.

Extensions

- How many more "original" facts could be added to the list beyond 100?
- The sticky-note facts could be arranged into categories (food, characteristics, predators, habitat). The children were fascinated by any information about baby penguins. Also, as students gathered information, they came to learn about different types of penguins, which suggested new categories.
- Students could brainstorm questions they have about penguins (perhaps using yet another color of sticky note). Further research could help students answer the questions.
- The class could create a collaborative book *What We Know About Penguins*, for which each student contributes one fact about penguins, accompanied by an illustration.

Bookshelf: Picture Books Featuring Penguins

Cowcher, Helen. *Antarctica*
Dunbar, Polly. *Penguin*
Fromental, Jean-Luc; illus. Joëlle Jolivet. *365 Penguins*
Jeffers, Oliver. *Lost and Found* (Also *Up and Down*)
John, Jory; illus. Lane Smith. *Penguin Problems*
London, Jonathan; illus. Julie Olson. *Little Penguin: The Emperor of Antarctica*
Minor, Wendell and Florence. *If You Were a Penguin*
Portis, Antoinette. *A Penguin Story*
Richardson, Justin and Peter Parnell; illus. Henry Cole. *And Tango Makes Three*
Watt, Mélanie. *Augustine*

What's the Big Idea?
An Integrated Approach to Social Studies and History

A "big idea" is an enduring understanding, an idea that we want students to delve into and retain long after they have forgotten many of the details of the content they studied. The big ideas address basic questions such as "Why am I learning this?" or "What is the point?"
—Ontario Ministry of Education, Social Studies, History and Geography, *Elementary Curriculum* (2013, p. 14)

Teachers continue to struggle with a very big question about teaching: With so much curriculum to cover, how can we teach the required curriculum in an engaging and thoughtful way, so that students move beyond learning content to think more critically and make meaningful connections? The concept of Big Ideas learning is one approach, a significant one, to support meaningful, authentic learning.

When students embark on Big Ideas curriculum, they become creators of their own understandings, not just passive receivers of facts and information. With Big Ideas curriculum, ideas, knowledge, and skills are transferable to a number of subjects. Moreover, Big Ideas provide students with opportunities to contemplate life experiences, issues, and possibilities.

📚 UNPACKING BIG IDEAS

Guest Voice: Helen Vlachoyannacos, Grade 7/8 Teacher

At the beginning of my career, I spent a lot of time teaching content, pushing students to learn facts, and regurgitating information about the social studies unit we were studying or the novel we were reading. Over the years, I've embarked on focusing my attention on making my teaching more intentional and purposeful for my students. In an age where they can Google everything and find factual information quite quickly, my focus needs to rest on facilitating learning that will allow students to question the world around them, thinking more deeply about issues they, and others in the world, face. I've come to realize that this responsibility lies with me, and it has changed the way I choose to teach—thinking about the texts I choose, the questions I ask, the prompts I state, and the opportunities I provide.

It was this realization that led me to begin planning in a more holistic manner, choosing a big idea or enduring understanding to organize my lessons around, threading in and connecting different curriculum expectations together. Choosing the big idea is an important step, as it needs to be something that students can relate to. This is easiest with the open-ended language and arts curricula; the difficult part is finding connections with the social studies or science curriculum. As a combined-grade teacher, I feel more compelled to plan in this way and set out to really focus on finding the cross-curriculum connections. Not only do I have the different subject expectations, but now I have to teach it to two grades. Overwhelming? Not with the integration of a big idea.

This year for Grade 7/8, I decided to think about integrating my history curriculum with my language and arts teaching. After much contemplation, I decided on the big ideas of *Struggle* and *Hope*. The notion of *struggle* seemed to connect to world history events from both the past and the present. Also, it is a word that I felt the young adolescents in my classroom could identify with. It was important to include the word "hope" in this investigation, since struggle and hope seem to go hand in hand: hope provides optimism and perseverance that students can contemplate when looking at historical events, personal experiences, and those drawn from literature. When I had this focus in hand, the pieces began to fall into place. I was able to choose texts that reflected this idea, and suddenly my history program on the development and creation of Canada came to life, going beyond learning in a rote way about events in Canada's history that students were disconnected from. The Big Ideas theme aroused students to go beyond history and consider current world events; it ignited students to make text-to-self connections to the fiction and nonfiction texts that would serve as a foundation for exploring Struggle and Hope.

Right from the beginning of the year, I ventured into working with the big idea, having students think about their own struggles and the way they have already shown resiliency and had hope. We talked about the hopes they have for the future and the goals and dreams they have for themselves, their community, and their world. Looking at key moments in their life allowed us to learn more about one another and create a caring community to work within for the year.

We then moved on to analyzing the struggles and hopes of characters with texts, including poems, media, scripts, and nonfiction and picture books. *Not My Fault* by Leif Kristiansson raises the question "Does this have anything to do with me?" *The Little Hummingbird* by Michael Nicoll Yahgulanaas presents the challenge of being passive or active participants ("I'm doing the best I can") when faced with struggle and conflict, and helped students create a personal sense of responsibility around how we deal with our own struggles and those of others. We used these opportunities to think critically about the struggles, and to analyze and synthesize what happened, why it happened, and the implications for social action. We talked about why we should care, why someone else's struggle should be something we spend time being hopeful about.

The story of Malala Yousafzai (*Every Day is Malala Day* by Rosemary McCarney) proved to be a pivotal resource to help us unpack and explode the theme: *Why should what happened to Malala Yousafzai be something we should think or care about?* Why should what happened, and continues to happen, to our Indigenous Peoples—residential schools and the missing and murdered Indigenous Women (*Missing Nimâmâ* by Melanie Florence)—be something students should think or care about? These two resources provided a significant turning point, as students came to reveal a great deal of empathy for different situations, allowing them to reflect and think about their role as global citizens, a key component of the social studies/history/geography curriculum.

We realized together that, through this learning and awareness, we can be the change makers. Combining education and social action, students can spread the word through their writing, through social media, through their art and music, through their choices. This took the learning to another level beyond simply trying to figure out marks and lesson plans. It created a space that allowed for students to become more strongly empathetic and caring, not because someone forced them to, but because they wanted to.

📚 SPOKEN WORD POEMS

Guest Voice: Helen Vlachoyannacos, Grade 7/8 Teacher

As the theme of Struggle and Hope unfolded, students found their voice to express their concerns, frustrations, sadness, hope. A significant connection in my writing program throughout this unit was engaging in spoken-word poetry study. I wanted students to channel their voices, to share all of their learning and all they were feeling. We launched into this study by familiarizing ourselves with and analyzing the form, after watching and listening to many examples. Poets, such as Prince Ea and Suli Breaks, filled our space, their words ringing off of the walls of our classroom; Sarah Kay's TED Talk, *If I Should Have a Daughter*, helped frame our own writing, as we used her techniques and prompts to write. "What are three things you know to be true, right now?" Sarah asks. We used this to begin our first written spoken-word piece.

The writing led to lessons around conventions of spoken-word poetry, like format and word choice. I worked with students in small groups, looking at topics they could relate to (e.g., pressures on a 13–14 year old), and we started drafting pieces together, then in small groups, then in pairs. All students, including struggling writers, were enthusiastic about this form of writing and the freedom it gave them. The performance element spoke to many students, and challenged some. As a community, we gently supported each other, as students understood that they needed to use their voice to share their passion about different issues or topics that they cared about.

Engaging in every learning opportunity allowed students to be active participants in the learning. On many occasions, students created the lesson plan and decided on where we were going to go next. And I was able to connect what was happening, what they were learning, to the expectations very easily. The context of the big idea helped to create a framework and set the stage for students to script and perform together, with me coaching and directing from backstage.

Bookshelf: Books on the Theme of Struggle and Hope

Picture Books

Florence, Melanie; illus. François Thisdale. *Missing Nimâmâ*
Kristiansson, Leif; illus. Dick Stenberg. *Not My Fault*
Skrypuch, Marsha Forchuk with Tuan Ho; illus. Brian Deines. *Adrift at Sea*
Walters, Eric; illus. Eugénie Fernandes. *Hope Springs*
Yahgulanaas, Michael Nicoll. *The Little Hummingbird*

Nonfiction

Arato, Rona. *The Ship to Nowhere*
Frier, Raphaëlle; illus. Aurélia Fronty. *Malala: Activist for Girls' Education*
Levine, Karen. *Hana's Suitcase*
McCarney, Rosemary. *Every Day is Malala Day*
Wilson, Janet. *Shannen and the Dream for a School*
Wilson, Janet. *Severn and the Day She Silenced the World*

Artful Responses:
Responding to Stories through Visual Arts

Many readers enjoy representing their responses visually. By drawing, painting, making models, or constructing collages, students—especially visual learners—can convey their ideas and feelings about a book they've read. Art provides a forum for students to express imagined thoughts.

For various reasons, including anxiety or difficulties with language, some readers are reluctant to respond orally or in writing. For these students, visual arts can offer a non-threatening opportunity to express their understanding and appreciation of what they read. Illustrations and other art projects can serve as artifacts for group discussion and can help others understand what a reader is saying about a book through the images, details, style, and emotions represented in the piece of art.

Responding to Picture Book Illustrations

1. How does the illustrator's choice of color(s) convey a mood or feeling?
2. What do you know about the medium (art style) used?
3. Do the illustrations give as much (or more) information as the verbal text?
4. Which illustration(s) do you think best matches the verbal text?
5. Which illustration might you like to own? Why?
6. Do you think each illustration is necessary? Explain
7. If you had to eliminate one illustration, which would you choose? Why?
8. If you could replace the cover image with another one from the book, which would you choose?
9. Is there an illustration you would have liked to see included that wasn't?
10. Draw a picture that you think would "continue" the book.

Five Art Responses to a Novel

1. Students design a character's room, showing furniture, books, souvenirs, and posters that represent the character's personality, interests, hobbies, and possessions.
2. Tell students to imagine they have been hired as an artist to create illustrations for a novel: *Which scenes painted a vivid picture in your mind? Which medium will you use to communicate your ideas?*
3. Students create a portrait mask for a character from a novel they've read. Students can cut out pictures from magazines or newspapers to represent events or symbols that reveal something about the character.
4. Film producers commission storyboards to help them structure the scenes in a film before it is shot. Students can create a storyboard showing a series of sketches representing plot highlights of one chapter or

sections of a novel. Sketches could represent the most powerful images that might appear if this novel were made into a film.

5. Students imagine that a novel is going to be made into a play or a film. The director requires a set to be constructed representing rooms or places described in the novel. Students create a diorama model set for one part of the novel.

VISUALIZING AND CREATING AN ILLUSTRATION

Larry visits Liza Taylor's Grade 3 Classroom

As we read, we are all illustrators-in-the head. An author's choice of words to tell a story, whether in picture-book or novel format, inspires readers to create still or moving images in their minds. The visual world that one reader creates will be very different from the one in the head of the person sitting beside them. Words can help us to capture ideas and feelings, but the machine of our imaginations is strengthened when we visualize a character, a setting, or an event from the text.

Asking our students to reveal what they see in their heads is an important meaning-making strategy. By providing materials and a context for students to pour those pictures onto paper, creating an illustration, or to construct or model what they are visualizing helps readers to bring forth and reveal their associations with written text. This should be something more than directing students to "draw a picture of their favorite scene." Visualization and illustration can work hand in hand when we encourage students to explicitly consider the author's words as well as to focus on the images that came to mind as they listened to or read a story, whether illustrations have already been included in the book or not.

In *The Gold Leaf* by Kirsten Hall, the animals of a forest are each tempted to own the single gold leaf that appears on a tree one spring day. A bird, a chipmunk, a squirrel, a deer, and a fox believe that they are deserving of this treasure and, because of their greed, the gold leaf is destroyed. The gold leaf images are presented in gold foil.

The picture book *The Gold Leaf* by Kirsten Hall was shared with students. As the book was read aloud, there was a conscious choice not to show all the illustrations that accompanied the verbal text. Students were encouraged to visualize what they imagined was taking place—the colors used and how the animals and trees might have been represented. After listening to the story, students were instructed to create an illustration that they think could have been included in the book. Students were also invited to create a picture that they think might have continued the story, which prompted students to visualize, make a prediction, and infer meaning. Students were instructed to create an illustration using construction paper and no scissors. The torn-paper medium challenged and delighted the students, who created some thoughtful, colorful images—each featuring a single gold leaf sticker.

The Sounds of Music: Integrating Literacy, Literature, and Music

Music and literature have strong connections, as they both can evoke powerful feelings, and involve imagination and creativity, and together they benefit both the cognitive and affective development of students. Literature has inspired many composers to write music that tells a story or paints a picture, empowering students to respond to what they hear by writing their own stories to express their thoughts, feelings, and ideas.

Oral language and reading connect with music as students add expression or sound effects to a chant, poem, or story, and as they perform a new interpretation of these works. Using a familiar text, students experience sound before symbol by clapping each syllable of the text. When they discover that the way the words go is actually the rhythm in music, students easily transition to reading the music symbols of rhythm. Literacy learning in language and music have many parallels and, when students can holistically experience them together, their application through creativity can be unleashed, so student voice can be heard.

Bookshelf: Sing a Book

Each of these books is based on a recorded song that will likely be familiar to students.

Beaumont, Karen; illus. David Catrow. *I Ain't Gonna Paint No More.*
Emberley, Ed and Rebecca. *If You're A Monster and You Know It.*
Lightfoot, Gordon; illus. Ian Wallace. *Canadian Railroad Trilogy*
Litwin, Eric; illus. James Dean. *Pete the Cat and His Four Groovy Buttons.*
Marley, Bob and Cedella; illus. Vanessa Brantley-Newton. *One Love*
Nelson, Kadir. *He's Got the Whole World in His Hands*
Raffi; illus. Nadine Bernard Westcott. *Down By The Bay* (Also *Shake My Sillies Out*; *The Wheels on the Bus*)
Seskin, Steve and Allen Shamblin; illus. Glin Dibley. *Don't Laugh At Me.*
Weiss, George David and Bob Thiele; illus. Tim Hopgood. *What a Wonderful World*
Williams, Pharrell. *Happy*

CREATING SOUNDSCAPES

Guest Voice: Jane Wamsley, Occasional Teacher

The activities presented here provide examples of integrating literature and music. When students create new works, their voices can resonate within their classroom, school, or wider community. These projects create interdependence in a group, as students collaborate, cooperate, and persevere from start to finish.

Peter and the Wolf

Several picture books are available that tell the story of *Peter and The Wolf*. Recent examples include versions by illustrator Chris Raschka and by Danila Vassilieff.

A recent active-listening experience with the popular music story *Peter and the Wolf* by Sergei Prokofiev invited Grade 4 students to explore the story as they learned about the timbres (distinct sounds) of the instruments and how the composer represents the character traits of the people and animals in the story. Students first moved their bodies to represent the character, then described how other music elements, such as rhythm, melody, and dynamics, were used by the composer to communicate the traits; e.g., the cat's sneaky music made up of low, long, smooth notes. Through repeated listening, students built a chart of how these music elements were combined by the composer. Students wrote a response about the most surprising, exciting, or dramatic part of the music, and how the composer's choices contributed to their feelings. Sharing ideas gave voice to how we interpret and feel music differently. Researching Prokofiev's historical times developed a cultural context.

Chalk by Bill Thomson

Students worked in groups of three or four. Each group was given a page from the wordless picture book *Chalk* by Bill Thomson. Each group created their own soundscape interpretation to animate the illustration. Sound sources they chose from included voices, body percussion, found sounds (e.g., chopsticks), non-pitched percussion (e.g., maracas), and pitched percussion instruments (e.g., xylophone). The groups were set in order in a circle and performed the story, flowing from one group to another, discovering together what the story was. Students were intrigued at how several of them articulated different interpretations of these soundscapes. Time for feedback, revising, and refining were given, and the "new" performance was shared with another class.

A student often shines unexpectedly in this process. As teachers, by learning more about our students' voices, we can offer integrated opportunities that will be effectively responsive to students' interests and needs.

SING A BOOK

Guest Voice: Jane Wamsley, Occasional Teacher

The Pharrell Williams song "Happy" was popular on the airwaves and many students were able to join in and sing the song aloud. When a picture-book version of Williams' song was published, students were given an opportunity to read the song that they were already familiar with. Many popular songs have been transformed into picture books. Many popular tunes (e.g., "If You're Happy and You Know It"; "It Ain't Gonna Rain No More!") are already ringing in children's heads, so experiencing a picture book in a read-aloud, shared reading, or independent read provides easy access and success to bring the words alive through voice.

Extension

Students can create their own picture-book version of a familiar song. Each student can contribute one page to accompany a line of text from the song. The illustrations can be assembled into a collaborative book for students to read and sing—a perfect integration of reading, music, and visual arts.

The following two documents, produced by the Elementary Teachers' Federation of Ontario, are a significant resource to help teachers integrate the arts in the literacy program:
• *Primary ETFO Arts: introducing, Dance, Drama, Music and Visual Arts in the Primary Grades,* 2013.
• *Revised ETFO Arts: introducing, Dance, Drama, Music and Visual Arts in the Junior Grades,* 2014.

Books that Move Me:
Integrating Literacy, Literature, and Dance

Traditionally, we respond to books through talk and writing. The arts also play a significant part, as students respond through visual arts, music, and drama activities. Dance is another way to respond. For many students, movement and dance ignites kinesthetic learning. Expressing ideas through body movement and gesture in space and time has an appeal for many students. Dance, with a language of its own, is a way to communicate ideas. When we integrate the dance curriculum with the language program, we are helping students develop an understanding and appreciation of dance. Literature can provide a context for physical nonverbal expression. We can give students opportunities to create works using the elements and choreographic forms of the discipline, opportunities to learn in kinesthetic, cognitive, and imaginative ways.

Bookshelf: Books on Dance and Movement

Andreae, Giles; illus. Guy Parker-Rees. *Giraffes Can't Dance*
Bluemie, Elizabeth; illus. Randy Cecil. *How do You Wokka-Wokka?*
Boynton, Sandra. *Dinosaurs Dance*
Dean, Kimberley and James. *Pete the Cat and the Cool Cat Boogie*
Emberley, Ed and Rebecca. *If You're A Monster and You Know It.*
Henson, T.R.; illus. Julie L. Casey. *I Can Dance, Can You?*
Jonas, Ann. *Color Dance*
Raffi; illus. David Allender. *Shake My Sillies Out.*
Walton, Rick; illus. Ana Lopez-Escriva. *How Can You Dance?*
Willems, Mo. *Elephants Cannot Dance!*

📚 DANCE A STORY

Guest Voice: Bonnie Anthony, Grade 4 Teacher

Moving Here and There

A favorite text to use in exploring movement, specifically the elements of space, relationship, shape, and level of the body, is the picture book *I'm Here* by Peter Reynolds. It is the story of a child on the Autism Spectrum, and provides an opportunity to discuss inclusion, exclusion, personal space, perspective, choice, and school playground dynamics. The ideas in the book prompt lessons that include movement by exploring and interpreting the sounds and movements of the playground that appear on the opening pages of the book, by becoming the airplane movements described in the book, and by using the words "I'm here!" to explore a vocabulary of dance that includes gesture, freezing, action, locomotor and non-locomotor movements, space, and time.

To begin, I started with a discussion of the cover of the book, inviting the students to discover where *here* and its opposite, *there*, might be. Playing with the concepts of here and there was a good springboard to body movement and special awareness, as students moved from *here* to *there* in a variety of ways: e.g., skipping, hopping, marching, etc.

Follow the Leader

1. I started as the leader and moved across the space in my classroom or an open room. I took on a frozen shape, saying, "I am here." Students approached slowly and quietly to where I was standing. They took on my shape and said, "Now I am here." Students remained frozen in space as I moved to another space in the room, posing in a new gesture and repeating, "Here I am!
2. Once the group understood the pattern, a student volunteer was chosen to be the leader. After they led a number of moves, the activity was modified to extend the learning.
3. Students worked in pairs, each having the opportunity to be the "I'm Here!" leader. Students were encouraged to move to different spaces and be inventive in their body poses and gestures.
4. The last step in this exploration invited the leader in each pair move to a space, take a frozen shape, and not say anything. The follower traveled to the leader and silently took the shape of the leader. The pattern continued, dropping the words but not the frozen shape.
5. Instrumental music was used to accompany the activity. Partners decided to interpret the music for movement and freezing into a position. This exploration modeled a way to move from word and movement to pure movement. Very quickly, the students had created a dance.

All in the Family: Responding Using Drama Conventions

In all grades, children's literature provides meaningful contexts for drama exploration. Drama, as a response mode, provides opportunities for students to step into the shoes of a character from a picture book, novel, script, biography, etc. to gain a better understanding of the character's dilemmas. By responding to literature through drama, readers can express a character's innermost thoughts and explore a text from a variety of viewpoints physically, orally, and in writing. When teachers use literature for drama experiences, they are integrating a medium that helps students develop an understanding of the art form, of themselves, and others, and that provides opportunities to learn about the lives of others in imagined contexts.

Our understandings of the complex, and often complicated, structures and definitions of family continue to expand as we all engage in learning about and through equity and diversity. Children's literature helps us to learn about diverse families by authors and illustrators creating rich stories about the lives and relationships between the characters in stories. Sometimes our students recognize the families in the stories as resembling their own, or they are able to make connections in meaningful ways. And other times, the families in the stories are a little (or a lot) different from their own families, or their conceptualization of *family*. Through illustrations and beautifully written stories about the ways in which families are structured and formed, children's literature teaches us about such diverse families as LGBTQ families, families with adopted children, extended families, families with one parent, families with multiple parents and siblings, families that face trauma and challenges, chosen families, and any combination of these.

Bookshelf: Books About Different Families and Gender Identity

Picture Books

De Haan, Linda and Stern Nijland. *King and King*

Elwin, Rosamund and Michele Paulse; illus. Dawn Lee. *Asha's Mums*

Hoffman, Mary; illus. Ros Asquith. *The Great Big Book of Families*

Newman, Leslea; illus. Carol Thompson. *Daddy, Papa, and Me*

Oelschlager, Vanita; illus. Kristin Blackwood and Mike Blanc. *A Tale of Two Daddies* (Also *A Tale of Two Mommies*)

Parr, Todd. *The Family Book*

Polacco, Patricia. *In Our Mothers' House*

Richardson, Justin and Peter Parnell; illus. Henry Cole. *And Tango Makes Three*

Setterington, Ken; illus. Alice Priestly. *Mom and Mum Are Getting Married*

Ware, Syrus Marcus. *Love Is in the Hair*

Novels

Donoghue, Emily; illus. Caroline Hadilaksono. *The Lotterys Plus One*

Peck, Richard. *The Best Man*

Peters, Julie Anne. *Between Mom and Jo*

DRAMA CONVENTIONS

A glossary of drama conventions appear in *This book is not about Drama... It's about new ways to inspire students* by Myra Barr, Bob Barton, and David Booth.

Guest Voice: Robert Durocher, Learning Coach, visits Ms. Lloyd's Grade 7/8 Classroom

In Patricia Polacco's *In Our Mothers' House* (2009), we meet Meema and Marmee, two lesbian mothers in a committed relationship, who adopt Will, Millie, and the narrator (the eldest), and we learn about their lives together as a family. The adopted children are of different racial identities, and this helps us further our learning around the ways that families look and are formed.

In Our Mothers' House not only facilitates discussions of who is in a family, but it also is a means to opening up discussions around adoption, interracial/transracial adoptions, and LGBTQ families. In the book, there is a point of tension as a neighbor confronts the family at a neighborhood event and vocalizes her dislike of and misunderstandings about the lesbian couple; this creates a point of discussion around homophobia and the ways in which some LGBTQ families are challenged and confronted with homophobic bullying and harassment. The story also lends itself to having discussions around the concept of home, where families live. While the family in the book faces confronting homophobia, they also have access to privilege in terms of socio-economic status, as demonstrated through the careers, the house, and the activities they engage in. In consideration of this, I have used *In Our Mothers' House* as a vehicle for discussions around the concept of *home*: where families live and the activities that they do in these spaces. It also has led to discussions around concepts of community and how families may feel when feel when included and excluded in a community. Moreover, using drama conventions, the students move into the world of pretend by becoming characters in the story; this helps them experience different points of view as they work inside the story.

In Ms. Lloyd's Grade 7/8 class, the lesson engaged the students in discussion of assumptions about families, of LGBTQ families and homophobia, of adoption, and of the ideas of home and community. To further our learning, I engaged in drama-based learning activities with students. Two drama conventions in particular helped me to further engage students in learning and conversing about equity and diversity of families.

Tableau with Thought Tracking

Two Tableaux

For more on tableaux, see the unit on Poverty, page 138.

The first activity engaged students in creating tableaux. To begin, students were instructed to depict one scene that explores the power dynamics summarized in the moment of tension when the family is confronted by the neighbor. I then had students create an additional tableau scene to depict what they thought might have happened after that scene (i.e., predicting how the problem was solved). The two tableaux provided opportunities to bring to life a moment in Polacco's narrative and to make a prediction about how the problem might have been solved (or not). The two tableaux were used for the next activity.

Thought Tracking

Thought Tracking (or Inner Voices) helps students become more aware of the complexity of a problem. As students are signaled to reveal their inner thoughts, they can become a character's conscience, consider moral or ethical choices, or add tension to the moment.

To further enrich the tableau scenes and dig deeper into the thoughts and feelings of the characters, the convention of thought tracking was introduced. I circulated through the groups and sporadically tapped students on the shoulder (or pointed to them). This was a prompt for them to consider the inner thoughts and feelings of the moms, neighbor, or children in a particular moment. On the signal, each student revealed their character's inner thoughts by articulating a statement or question about the character's feelings and concerns. This activity invited students to track the thoughts of the character at the same time as it provided a drama structure to explore the impact of homophobia on members of family and community members.

Collective Character: Interviewing in Role

An additional activity involved getting to know the narrator by taking the roles of other people in the story or those who are not featured in Polacco's narrative but might be connected to the narrator's life. For this activity, students worked in groups of two or three to collectively work in role as a character (e.g., teacher, friend, birth parent that gave her up for adoption, LGBTQ family support worker, etc.) With Collective Character work, more than one person simultaneously assumes one role. Any one of the participants can speak as the character being portrayed.

Once students decided which character they would collectively choose to role-play, the group brainstormed questions they might ask the narrator in order to unpack her story, her attitude, and her connections to the family relationship described in the story. Students next were invited to use their questions to interview the narrator, with me in the role. I circulated through the space and, as I approached a group, group members could ask questions that would reveal stories about the narrator character. Following the interview, a final discussion was conducted to consider what new information we learned about the character, what new questions we might ask the character, and how the problem was solved (or not) for the mothers, the children, and the neighbors. I asked students: "What would you do in this situation?" "What events from your own life or from the life of someone you know does this remind you of?" Finally, I asked students to define a family and helped them to consider the big idea connected to *In Our Mothers' House*.

As I engaged with students through drama activities based on *In Our Mothers' House*, I feel that the learning came through inquiring and exploring family dynamics through drama. Students not only learned about different formations of family, they also learned about the ways in which homophobia and heteronormativity affect the lives of LGBTQ families.

Possible Extensions

- Writing in Role: In-role journal as a character in the story, reflecting on the views and feelings that that character might have experienced.
- Media: Students can work in small groups to create a Public Service Announcement (PSA), YouTube video, or informational brochure around the theme of diversity. To prepare for the activity, students can view equity- and social-justice–themed media texts and co-create anchor charts and success criteria around what makes media texts effective in delivering their messages.

Professional Resources

General Resources

Allen, Janet (2000) *Yellow Brick Roads: Shared and Guided Paths to Independent Reading, 4-12.* Portland, ME: Stenhouse.

Allen, Janet and Patrick Daley (2004) *The Scholastic Read-aloud Anthology: 35 short, riveting read-alouds that build comprehension, listening and higher level thinking skills—and keep kids on the edge of their seats.* New York, NY: Scholastic.

— (2017) *Riveting Read-Alouds for Middle School.* New York, NY: Scholastic.

Atwell, Nancie (2007) *The Reading Zone: How to Help Kids Become Skilled, Passionate, Habitual, Critical Readers.* New York, NY: Scholastic.

Barr, Myra, Bob Barton, and David Booth (2012) *This book is not about Drama… It's about new ways to inspire students.* Markham, ON: Pembroke.

Booth, David (2011) *Caught in the Middle: Reading and Writing in the Transition Years.* Markham, ON: Pembroke.

— (2002) *Even Hockey Players Read.* Markham, ON: Pembroke.

— (2016) *Literacy 101.* Markham, ON: Pembroke.

Booth, David and Bob Barton (2004) *Poetry Goes to School.* Markham, ON: Pembroke.

Booth, David, and Bill Moore (2003) *Poems Please!* Markham, ON: Pembroke.

Booth, David, and Kathleen Gould Lundy (2007) *In Graphic Detail: Using Graphic Novels in the Classroom.* Oakville, ON: Rubicon.

Booth, David, and Larry Swartz (2006) *Learning to Read with Graphic Power.* Oakville, ON: Rubicon.

Daniels, Harvey (2002) *Literature Circles, 2nd Edition: Voice and Choice in Book Clubs and Reading Groups.* Portland, ME: Stenhouse.

Denby, David (2016) *Lit Up: One Reporter. Three Schools. Twenty-four books that can change lives.* New York, NY: Henry Holt & Co.

Donohue, Lisa (2015) *Independent Reading Inside the Box, 2nd Edition.* Markham, ON: Pembroke.

Dufflemeyer, F. (1994) "Effective Anticipation Guide statements for learning from expository prose" *Journal of Reading*, 37, 452–455.

Elementary Teachers' Federation of Ontario (2013) *Primary ETFO Arts: Introducing Dance, Drama, Music and Visual Arts in the Primary Grades.*

— (2014) *Revised ETFO Arts: Introducing, Dance, Drama, Music and Visual Arts in the Junior/Intermediate Grades.*

— (2011) *More Than a Play.*

Engel, Susan (1995) *The Stories Children Tell: Making Sense of the Narratives of Childhood.* New York, NY: Henry Holt.

Foster, Graham (2012) *Ban the Book Report.* Markham, ON: Pembroke.

Fox, Mem; illus. Judy Horacek (2008) *Reading Magic: Why Reading Aloud to Our Children Will Change Their Lives Forever, 2nd ed.* New York, NY: Harcourt.

Gear, Adrienne (2015) *Reading Power, Revised & Expanded Edition.* Markham, ON: Pembroke.

— (2008) *Nonfiction Reading Power.* Markham, ON: Pembroke.

— (2011) *Writing Power.* Markham, ON: Pembroke.

— (2014) *Nonfiction Writing Power.* Markham, ON: Pembroke.

Heard, Georgia (2013) *Finding the Heart of Nonfiction.* Portsmouth, NH: Heinemann.

Kittle, Penny (2012) *Book Love: Developing Depth, Stamina and Passion in Adolescent Readers.* Portsmouth, NH: Heinemann.

Koechlin, Carol, and Sandi Zwaan (2014) *Q Tasks, 2nd Edition.* Markham, ON: Pembroke.

Landt, Susan (2006) "Multicultural literature and young adolescents: A kaleidoscope of opportunity" *Journal of Adolescent & Adult Literacy,* 49, 690–697.

Layne, Steven (2015) *In Defense of Read-Aloud: Sustaining Best Practice.* Portland, ME: Stenhouse Publishers.

Lundy, Kathy Gould (2015) *Conquering the Crowded Curriculum.* Markham, ON: Pembroke.

Lundy, Kathy Gould, and Larry Swartz (2011) *Creating Caring Classrooms.* Markham, ON: Pembroke.

Maliszewski, Diana (2013) "The Benefits of Writing Comics" pp. 233–235 in Carrye Kay Syma and Robert G. Weiner (eds.). *Graphic Novels and Comics in the Classroom: Essays on the Educational Power of Sequential Art.* Jefferson, NC: McFarland.

Miller, Donalyn (2009) *The Book Whisperer: Awakening the Inner Reader in Every Child.* San Francisco, CA: Jossey-Bass.

Miller, Donalyn with Susan Kelley (2013) *Reading in the Wild: The Book Whisperer's Keys to Cultivating Lifelong Reading Habits.* San Francisco, CA: Jossey-Bass.

Morgan, Norah, and Juliana Saxton (2006) *Asking Better Questions, 2nd Edition.* Markham, ON: Pembroke.

Ontario Ministry of Education (2013) *Elementary Curriculum.*

Peterson, Shelley Stagg. (2010) *Teaching with Graphic Novels.* Winnipeg, MB: Portage and Main.

Peterson, Shelley Stagg, and Larry Swartz (2008) *Good Books Matter.* Markham, ON: Pembroke.

— (2015) *"This is a Great Book!"* Markham, ON: Pembroke.

Schwalbe, Will (2016) *Books for Living.* New York, NY: Alfred A. Knopf.

Schwartz, Susan, and Mindy Polishuke (2017) *Creating the Dynamic Classroom, 3rd edition.* Toronto, ON: Pearson Canada.

Silvey, Anita (2009) *Everything I Need to Know I Learned from a Children's Book.* New York, NY: Roaring Brook Press.

Stead, Tony (2009) *Good Choice! Supporting Independent Reading and Response K-6*. Portland, ME: Stenhouse.

Swartz, Larry (2014) *Dramathemes, 4th edition*. Markham, ON: Pembroke.

— (2000) *Text Talk: Towards an Interactive Classroom Model for Encouraging, Supporting and Promoting Literacy*. Thesis dissertation.

— (2006) *The Novel Experience*. Markham, ON: Pembroke.

— (2009) *The Picture Book Experience*. Markham, ON: Pembroke.

Swartz, Larry and Sheree Fitch (2008) *The Poetry Experience*. Markham, ON: Pembroke.

Szymusiak, Karen, Franki Sibberson, and Lisa Koch (2008) *Beyond Leveled Books*. Portland, ME: Stenhouse.

Thompson, Terry (2008) *Adventures in Graphica: Using Comics and Graphic Novels to Teach Comprehension, 2–6*. Portland, ME: Stenhouse.

Trelease, Jim (2013) *The Read-Aloud Handbook, 7th edition*. New York, NY: Penguin.

Wilhelm, Jeffrey D., Peggy Jo Wilhelm, and Erika Boas (2009) *Inquiring Minds: Learn to Read and Write: 50 Problem-Based Literacy & Learning Strategies*. Oakville, ON: Rubicon.

Issues and Subjects

Gender Issues

Kuklin, Susan (2015) *Beyond Magenta: Transgender Teens Speak Out*. Somerville, MA: Candlewick Press.

Duron, Lori (2013) *Raising My Rainbow: Adventures in Raising a Fabulous, Gender Creative Son*. New York, NY: Broadway Books.

Bullying

Beane, A. L. (2005) *The Bully Free Classroom*. Minneapolis, MN: Free Spirit.

Coloroso, B. (2003) *The Bully, The Bullied, Bystander*. Toronto, ON: HarperCollins.

— (2005) *Just Because It's Not Wrong Doesn't Make it Right: From toddlers to teens, teaching kids to think and act ethically* Toronto, ON: Viking.

Daniels, Harvey and Sara K. Ahmed. (2014) *Upstanders: How to Engage Middle School Hearts and Minds with Inquiry*. Portsmouth, NH: Heinemann.

Henkin, R. (2005) *Confronting Bullying: Literacy as a tool for character education*. Portsmouth, NH: Heinemann.

Hirsch, L & C. Lowen (2012) *Bully: An action plan for teachers, parents, and communities to combat the bullying crisis*. New York, NY: Weinstein.

Lundy, Kathy Gould, and Larry Swartz (2011) *Creating Caring Classrooms*. Markham, ON: Pembroke.

Paley, V.G. (1992) *You Can't Say, You Can't Play*. Cambridge, MA: Harvard University Press.

Rigby, Ken (2001) *Stop the Bullying: A handbook for teachers*. Markham, ON: Pembroke.

Swartz, Larry (2013) *The Bully-Go-Round*. Markham, ON: Pembroke.

Math

Boaler, Jo (2015) *Mathematical Mindsets: Unleashing Students' Potential through Creative Math, Inspiring Messages and Innovative Teaching.* Etobicoke, ON: John Wiley & Sons.

Fiore, Mary and Maria Luisa Lebar (2016) *The Four Roles of the Numerate Learner.* Markham, ON: Pembroke.

Marks Krpan, Cathy (2013) *Math Expressions: Developing Student Thinking and Problem Solving Through Communication.* Toronto, ON: Pearson.

— (2017) *Teaching Math with Meaning: Cultivating Self-efficacies Through Learning Competencies.* Toronto, ON: Pearson.

Parrish, Sherry (2014) *Number Talks: Helping Children Build Mental Math and Computation Strategies, Grades K–5.* Toronto, ON: Pearson.

Siena, Maggie (2009) *From Reading to Math: How Best Practices in Literacy can Make You a Better Math Teacher.* Orlando, FL: Math Solutions.

Small, Marian (2013) *Eyes on Math: A Visual Approach to Teaching Math Concepts (K-8).* Toronto, ON: Nelson

Mentor Texts

Culham, R. and J. Blasingame (2010) *Using Mentor Texts to Teach Writing with the Traits: Middle School.* New York, NY: Scholastic.

Dorfman, Lynne R. and R. Cappelli (2017) *Mentor Texts: Teaching Writing through Children's Literature, K–6, 2nd edition.* Portland, ME: Stenhouse.

Dorfman, Lynne R. and R. Cappelli (2009) *Nonfiction Mentor Texts: Teaching Informational Writing through Children's Literature, K–8.* Portland, ME: Stenhouse.

Index